Brave Tales

Developing Literacy through
Storytelling

Will Coleman

network
continuum

Published by Network Continuum Education
The Tower Building
11 York Road
London
SE1 7NX

www.networkcontinuum.co.uk
www.continuumbooks.com

An imprint of The Continuum International Publishing Group Ltd

First published 2007
© Will Coleman 2007

ISBN-13: 978 1 85539 225 0
ISBN-10:   1 85539 225 9

Design and layout by: Neil Hawkins, ndesignuk.co.uk
Illustrations by: Kerry Ingham, Will Coleman (pages 31–33, 117 and 136)

Printed in Great Britain by MPG Books Ltd, Bodmin, Cornwall

Contents

Foreword   4

About this book   5

Chapter 1 **Storytelling**

Why storytelling?   7

Once upon a time…   9

What do good storytellers do?   10

Doesn't writing matter most?   12

Does storytelling improve writing?   16

Chapter 2 **Storyboarding**

Lost the plot?   21

What are storyboards?   23

Creating storyboards   26

The uses of storyboards   34

Transforming stories   37

Chapter 3 **Speaking and listening**

What do good listeners do?   45

Speaking and listening   49

Listening partners   52

Feedback and coaching   58

Chooser boards   62

Chapter 4 **Creativity**

The ideas factory   71

Collaborative creativity   80

Collaborative storytelling   85

Tableaux   87

Role play   91

Chapter 5 **Writing**

Principles for an effective writing culture   97

Headlines and bullet points   104

Aural preparation for writing   117

Interactive writing   120

Writing frames   126

Conclusion   133

An afterthought: storytelling for non-fiction and across the curriculum   135

References   138

Index   140

Foreword

Down here in Cornwall, they know about stories – there are tales of a giant at St Michael's Mount, a mermaid at Zennor, pale-faced piskies dodging through the darkness of the ancient mines...

And no one knows more than Will Coleman. A modern-day Cornish giant – Bard of the Gorsedd, actor, author, teacher – he's been telling stories to children in Cornish schools for 20 years. He knows all the secrets, including that most magical secret of all – how to open children's ears and minds to the power of words.

To become literate, children must be able to *listen* – to pick up the patterns and rhythms of sentences, to acquire a store of words for exploring and expressing ideas. But in today's multimedia world, listening has been sidelined. Contemporary children get their stories on screen – images, colour, light... few words, just odd scraps of dialogue and sound effects. If we want to put words, sentences and text into their heads, it's essential that we revive the art of storytelling.

So forget national documents, strategies and government guidelines. If you want to teach your class to write, listen hard to the genuine wisdom in this book. Get your class acting, making, drawing, telling stories. Help them listen to the lilt of the sentences, ponder on the weight of the words, tussle towards the best possible telling of a tale.

This is a book to savour and enjoy, written by a master-teacher and storyteller, rooted in a true understanding of children, language and learning. And like all the best teaching, it's fun. If you follow Will Coleman's advice, you'll not only teach literacy through storytelling – you and your class will have an absolutely wonderful time.

Sue Palmer
Truro, 2007

About this book

Hello!

Welcome to this book.

The intention of *Brave Tales* is that the contents are both thought provoking and immediately useful. We will find ourselves questioning what literacy is all about at a basic level, but there are also plenty of activities that can be used straight away that you might like to try in the classroom (or out of it) tomorrow morning.

This book is arranged so that you can start at the beginning and go straight through to the end. This is because a 'dip-in' book of handy ideas could leave you missing the more important *principles* that underpin the approach.

However, if you find reading anything in a logical sequence a nightmare chore, I give you permission to dip. Just promise me that you will not put your pupils through these activities unless you know why you are doing them!

Because it is difficult to describe a storytelling session accurately, I have included a DVD that shows me telling *Little Red Riding Hood* to a Key Stage 2 class. Of course, it would be far better if you were to engage the services of a stalwart local storyteller or, better still, jump in and tell it yourself!

Have fun

Will Coleman

Chapter **1**

Storytelling

▶ Why storytelling?

Begin by pulling a memory to the fore. When did you last read a story to someone else? The class? A group? Your little one at home? Can you remember what that felt like? Where exactly were you? Who was the 'audience'? What was going on for you, between you, or for them?

Now, can you contrast that with a second memory – when was the last time you closed a book and told someone a story?

Brave Tales is not an anti-book book! Our job is to turn young people on to the fabulous wealth of wonderful books that exist, but we are going to explore what happens when you tell a story *without* a book.

- Perhaps you tell stories to your class every day – for some reason that's more likely if you teach Foundation or Key Stage 1.

- Perhaps you tell a story now and again in assembly – why do we feel more confident if we're working towards a highly 'moral' conclusion?

- Perhaps you claim that you never tell stories – how about gossiping in the staffroom, relating embarrassing incidents or hard-luck yarns?

Now, if we contrast these experiences, we can pose the question: Why *storytelling*?

What is it about the experience of sharing a story orally or verbally that makes it so special? Most people, quite instinctively, come up with a whole raft of reasons that could be summarized something like the diagram below.

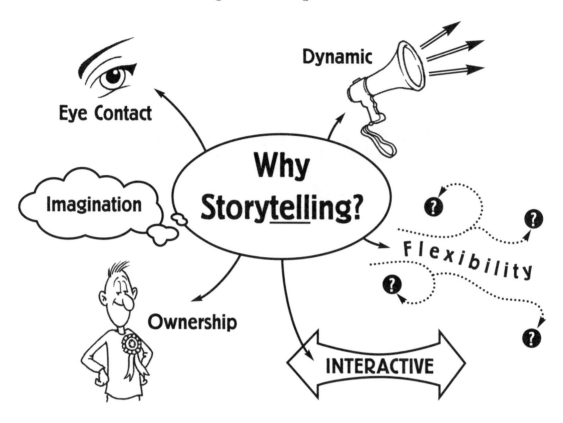

Eye contact   Without a book forming a barrier 'twixt teller and audience, it is possible to share the experience around and make sure that everyone gets a bit. People become engaged and attentive, and behaviour management issues evaporate (they really do!).

Dynamic   Why should holding a book 'calm down' your performance so much? I don't know, but it does. Suddenly, without a book, tellers will leap and hoot, gesticulate and become the characters in the story.

Imagination   Telling a story places greater demands on the teller's imagination – much more so than reading someone else's words. Appropriate levels of demand are good for us! The skilful part is to keep the level of challenge stretching but not so daunting as to intimidate and lead to failure (more of that later).

The audience, too, are challenged to visualize and imagine. We will explore ways to deliberately practise and develop our visualization skills. After all, as Granny said, 'You get the best pictures on the radio!'

Flexibility   People often assume that storytelling means 'improvising a brand new story, making it up as you go along'. Well, storytelling can mean that, and storytelling can be flexible at the plot level. However, for various reasons, that is a high-order skill. So, in the first instance, we are talking about flexibility in detail, content, timing, pitch, delivery and style. The story itself can be a tried and tested, well-known, well-loved classic. The point is that even the most well-worn story can be refreshingly personalized.

Ownership   As a child, a teacher told me that someone had written each of the books in the library. 'No way,' I thought – my five-year-old world couldn't cope with that many authors scribbling away. I thought they came from a factory. Storytelling sidesteps the distant, worthy (and sometimes long dead) author to bring the act of creation to 'right here, right now'. You can switch on young people to the wonders of all manner of great authors but, first of all, how about your creating something worthwhile – here and now?

To sum all this up:

Storytelling is interactive!

Audience and teller collaborate in a two-way experience that is immediate, unique and personal.

So, let me tell you a story, so that we've got an example to base our work on and so that we can discuss the nature of the beast.

▶ Once upon a time...

Just before you slip the *Little Red Riding Hood* DVD into your machine, here's a task for you to do while listening to the story: look out for 'tricks' that demonstrate the storyteller's techniques. While listening, you will certainly be using your imagination to visualize the various characters, scenes and events. Also try to imagine what you would be getting additionally from a live storyteller. These are the extras that add to a retelling as opposed to a 'reading'.

Did you enjoy that? We shall be referring back to Little Red as an example throughout the book, although all the activities work with whichever story you choose to use.

Did you spot some storytelling techniques? In other words, can you answer the question: What do good storytellers do?

▶ What do good storytellers do?

The quality of responses to this question, even from young children, is often impressive.

Collected and tidied up their answers could look like this:

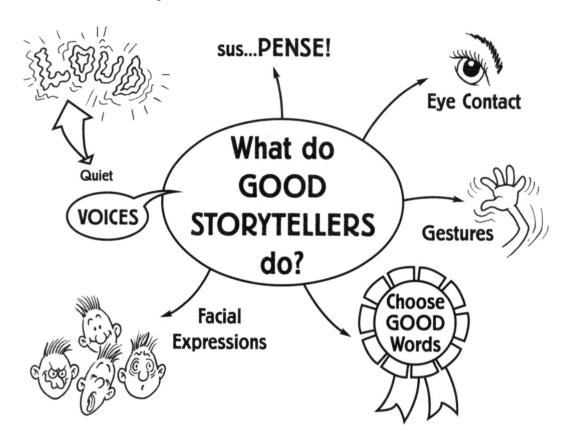

Now we have created a success criteria chart. Put it up on the classroom wall, as big and colourful as possible, and refer back to it every time you want dynamic, interactive storytelling.

Eye contact Hard to demonstrate this on a DVD, but kids really do notice that you are speaking directly to them. Be careful not to sweep or glance around your audience but pick out random individuals and treat them to a phrase or even a whole sentence each!

Voices Putting on the characters' voices is, of course, a major piece of storytelling decorative art. It's also fun to play with dynamics, not just getting loud and booming but also seeing how small and soft you can go, pulling the focus right in.

Gestures Freed from book holding, your hands (and the rest of your body) are available to add detail. You do not have to go into full-blown mime – a grip on the handle of the basket, claws displayed when the Wolf is revealed, a glance around the Dark Woods, all work wonders.

Facial expressions   To complete the sense of becoming the character, the audience want to read the emotion from your facial clues. Try endowing each character with a very simple attribute; for example, Little Red with eyebrows up and eyes wide, Wolf with nostrils flared and sardonic smile. These attributes can be understated but they serve to differentiate the characters well. Similarly, you can have a directional difference; for example, Little Red always speaks up and to the left, Wolf speaks down and to the right.

Sus...pense!

It is surprisingly easy to find moments in a story where you can pause and leave the audience in suspense. The more they want to hear the next bit, the longer you can milk the 'revelation'.

There was rustle and a quiver, third bush from the left … the crack of a twig … someone or something was watching and waiting … suddenly Little Red's nostrils were assailed by a pungent doggy aroma…

Similarly, if you do have a prop to go with the story, you don't have to reveal it straight away. Keep it back, peer into the bag, or box, with delight, and engage the audience's curiosity. You can produce even a crumpled up crisp packet with such reverence that they will be convinced it is magical!

Choose good words   This is important. It is so important that many teachers get their carts before their horses and allow it to become more vital than the plot/storyline. Well, it's not that important!

Later, we will explore how to choose good words, once we have established a confident structure to work within. There is a great deal we can do to support the choosing of good words.

Teachers as storytellers – asking too much?

Are you feeling too nervous to actually put down the book and *tell* a story to your class of hairy Year 5s! Why? What if you go wrong, lose the plot, fail to entertain or amuse? Will you endanger or even lose your 'hard won, high status' as a teacher?

Well, I was teaching for more than two years before I finally picked up the courage to simply tell my pupils a traditional story. Instantly, I couldn't think why I had waited so long. My telling was not perfect by any means, but the pupils supported, encouraged and helped me through it. They loved it! From then on I began using storytelling on a regular basis.

Every time you tell your pupils a new story, it feels as though you have given them another little gift. Call me an old hippy if you like, but I believe that storytelling will do as much for the social/behavioural climate of your class as will all your circle time and other PSHE endeavours. There's *love* in storytelling.

So, understandably, taking the leap into storytelling may be pretty daunting for many of us. But, never fear, support structures, 'edge-your-way-in' ideas, beginners' scaffolds will all be revealed in later chapters.

So, could you be brave enough to have a go at storytelling yourselves. Facial expressions – you can do that. Gestures – no problem. Voices – have a go. In fact, you can already do everything that's on the 'Good storytellers' spider gram. So what's stopping you from leaping in and telling your story?

It is probably because you are still worried that you might lose your way, forget what comes next or miss an important bit out. You see, everything on the 'Good storytellers' spider gram is just icing on the cake. None of it is essential. What is essential is a good cake to put the icing on to and a good story to work with.

What you need is a tool with which to understand, learn and remember the plot of your story. What you need is a STORYBOARD!

At this point, you can jump to Chapter 2, 'Storyboarding' (page 21) if you want some practical suggestions for classroom activities. Or, to gain a deeper insight into some of the thinking behind the storytelling approach, read on.

▶ Doesn't writing matter most?

Consider the following points:

- Our society assumes a basic ability in writing for adults – without such ability many doors are closed.

- Any pupil trying to make their way through secondary education (as currently practised in Britain) without a reasonably fluent writing ability is most likely doomed to struggle.

- A primary school can expect to have its entire range of achievement reduced to a league-table place based on how well last year's cohort of 11 year olds did at writing.

So, surely what really matters is *writing*?

Probably the best way to tackle this is to go back to basics and re-open the question: What do we mean by *Literacy*?

Literacy – the National Curriculum, of course, does not mention 'Literacy'. It talks about *English*. (Are Welsh speakers not literate? Is it possible or valuable to develop literacy through Urdu or French, not just through English?)

The National Literacy Strategy (1999) told us the official view:

What is Literacy? Literacy unites the important skills of reading and writing. It also involves speaking and listening.

Have we got our priorities right here?

Let's ask ourselves how many times we have 'been literate' today? Yesterday? How often do we need to 'be literate' every week to get through or to be successful in life?

Try making a spider gram of all the tasks that involve literacy every day/week. Most people's spider gram begins a bit like the following:

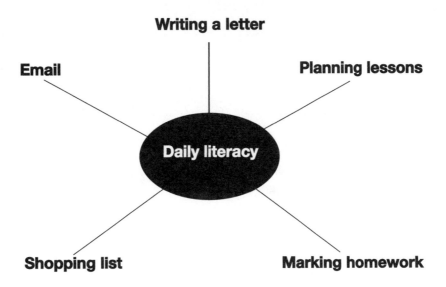

Which all involve writing.

The spider grams could perhaps develop a bit like this:

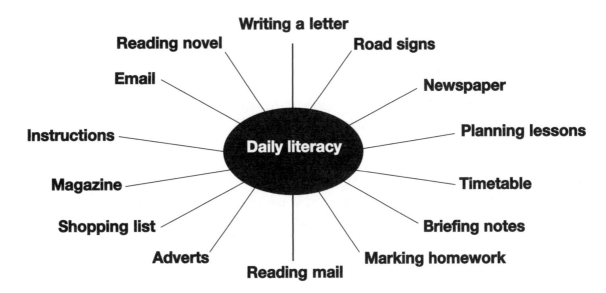

Which all involve reading.

Finally, we get:

Which all involve speaking and listening.

The above spider grams are by no means exhaustive and will be significantly different for many – especially those of us with particular sensory requirements. The point is, as a simplified generalization, if we had to do without one of the three accomplishments (reading, writing, or speaking and listening), which would have the most profound impact on our lives?

The answer is speaking and listening – we use these with much greater frequency. There are many adults in our society unable to write. They have a tough time, but they get through. Those unable to read have it even tougher. Whereas adults who, for whatever reason, have never developed the ability to speak or listen have an enormously difficult time participating in society at all.

In fact, the breadth of activities in these spider grams leads us towards a new definition of 'Literacy'; perhaps literacy is simply the skill with which we communicate. So, that would mean: yes, you can develop your literacy through Welsh, Urdu, British Sign Language, Braille, drawing pictures, Makaton, Give-Us-a-Clue, ICT and so on.

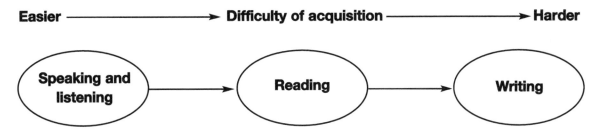

● Usual order of literacy acquisition/proficiency

There is a sense of development here running left to right. How many pupils have you had who were proficient in writing yet poor at speaking and listening? They do exist but are clearly exceptions to the rule. In general, we might hypothesize that a solid proficiency in speaking and listening is a necessary precursor to both reading and writing.

None of this is rocket science; in fact, it's just common sense. Yet, every day in our schools, how many teachers are banging their heads against the wall, desperately trying to force written work out of pupils who are barely able to string a coherent spoken sentence together? The answer is many. The written outcome is seen as the only legitimate goal and essential building blocks are simply ignored.

We often hear that pupils have no culture of reading in the home; they do not see their parents reading for leisure and rarely see them reading out of necessity. Thus, they cannot see the point of reading; they have no understanding of its usefulness or its possibilities.

How much more profound again is the writing deficit? Very few of us sit down and write for enjoyment. Very few pupils have ever seen their parents writing for any reason. Yet we expect our children to understand the importance of and be motivated to master the complicated set of skills involved.

I would like to add two more bubbles to the left-hand end of our literacy continuum.

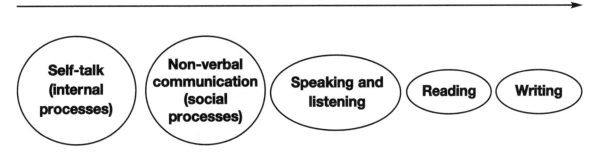

● Usual order of literacy acquisition/proficiency with earliest stages added

We're now venturing somewhat beyond the promised scope of this book and we had better not go off at great length.

However, when there's a problem at one level, it is often necessary to dig to a deeper level in order to remedy it. We hardly ever explicitly teach 'How to think about ourselves' or 'How to let people know how you are feeling non-verbally'. But these skills, too, underpin literacy and, thankfully, more practitioners are becoming aware of the issues.

Now to the main issue.

▶ Does storytelling improve writing?

Later in this book, we will consider deconstruction of the writing process and make some specific suggestions regarding 'How to teach writing'. However, in the short term, here is an outrageous claim:

Even if you do NOT teach any writing skills explicitly, then simply through storytelling alone your pupils' written outcomes will improve!

Want it again, even simpler?

Just do storytelling and their writing will improve!

What possible authority can there be for such a claim?

Recently, Brave Tales Ltd carried out some action research for the newly formed Camborne Pool and Redruth Education Action Zone, which had requested a 'Developing Literacy through Storytelling Project' (www.bravetales.com).

The brief was something like 'We obviously care deeply about the long-term social and emotional welfare of our pupils, but in the short-term, can you come in and do some drastic emergency work on increasing our poor Y6 SATs results?'.

In a nutshell, we took ten Y6 classes and asked all 300 pupils to write a mock SATs task, which we marked, levelled and moderated. Leaving five classes to get on with their own work, we engaged with the other five classes, working with teachers, teaching assistants and pupils to build a story-telling culture. After four months, they all wrote us another story. Opposite are the graphs we produced to show the impact.

So, without any specific input on writing, our sample showed very significant improvement on their writing outcomes. Why? First and foremost, because the pupils were engaged and motivated. With these key aspects in place, children will learn like sponges, tackle huge obstacles, and succeed, sometimes in spite of unhelpful teaching practices. Without engagement and motivation, the whole enterprise is on a hiding to nothing – teachers are pushing it uphill, kids are resisting, everyone and everything spirals into despondency. So here's the good news:

Storytelling is both fun and effective – for teachers and for pupils!

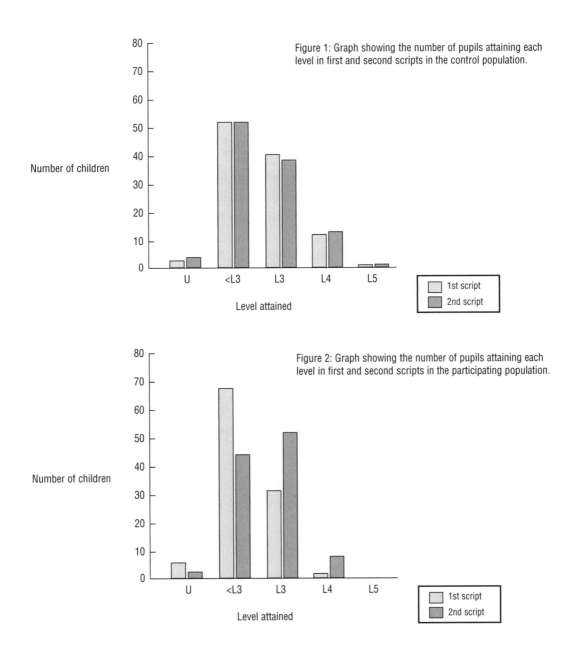

Figure 1: Graph showing the number of pupils attaining each level in first and second scripts in the control population.

Figure 2: Graph showing the number of pupils attaining each level in first and second scripts in the participating population.

If it's not fun, what is the point?

Of course, it is not quite as simple as that. 'Just have fun' sounds like the 'Happy Hippy Hopeful' school of pedagogy. It is possibly true that if we had gone into those (socially depressed, rather unloved and overlooked) classes in the 'Success Zone' and taught them all to juggle and ride unicycles, their story-writing would still have improved (it couldn't have got worse!). But, we are all bringing a little more rigour to our practice these days and our intervention was somewhat more targeted than most. However, we do not have to subscribe to the school of thought that says 'learning must be a struggle' or 'no pain, no gain'. One Year 6 teacher told me: 'They'll have to sit in rows and work in silence at the secondary school, so they might as well get used to it now!' I imagined the secondary school teacher adding: 'They won't be having any fun when they're out in the real world of work, so they might as well get used to it now!' There are, of course, certain times when sitting in rows and working in silence is exactly the appropriate thing to do. The point is that the young people in our care deserve life-enriching, stimulating, purposeful experiences. They deserve fun! You never know, if they come to equate hard work *with* fun, realize that the two go hand in hand and expect fun/hard work as a daily experience, they might even grow up into delightful, industrious, socially responsible and engaging adults!

There's more to stories than just fun

There has never been a human culture or civilization that did not have Story at the core of its cultural complex. Perhaps in our modern-day Western society, we think that we no longer need such an 'outdated' manifestation of our 'primitive' past?

Yet, take away Story from films, TV programmes or gossip and it's a strange, cultural void that might remain. Yes, gossiping is a much overlooked and underrated activity. Gossip has traditionally received bad press from the 'powers that be' and has been given negative connotations. However, in practice, we find that good gossipers enjoy very high social standing among their peers and, as educators, empowering young people to be articulate, constructive gossipers is an extremely laudable objective.

It appears that Story is hard-wired into the human brain. Again and again across cultures and millennium, the same plot structures and motives arise (see Booker, 2004).

How do we know when a mere anecdote has become a proper *story*? Why do some plots uplift us and help us feel recharged, while others leave us feeling curiously unsatisfied?

Why fairytales?

When you first begin working with traditional tales, you may feel somewhat troubled about the amount of cliché that appears to be going on. Helpless princesses rescued by perfect Prince Charmings seem to have no place in a modern post-feminist, multicultural classroom.

All those happy endings – aren't you tempted to take them down a peg or two, insert a bit more grit. After all, life's not like that – is it?

But, a big change came over me on reading *The Uses of Enchantment* by Bruno Bettelheim, who made me entirely rethink what stories are for. He says:

On an overt level fairy tales teach little about the specific conditions of life in a modern mass society ... But more can be learned from them about the inner problems of human beings, and of the right solutions to their predicaments in any society, than from any other type of story.
(Bettelheim, 1976)

Bettelheim seems to mean that Story is an essential part of our psychological development. Each of those characters in the stories represents a different aspect of ourselves and helps us gain understanding at a subconscious psychological level.

Just in case Bettelheim's approach is a little too esoteric for you, it could be expressed more simply:

Stories are Medicine.
(Clarissa Pinkola Estes, 1992)

… and just in case you haven't read Estes and require a more familiar authority, how about:

If you want brilliant children, tell them fairytales.
(attributed to Albert Einstein)

Chapter **2**

Storyboarding

▶ Lost the plot?

When you analyse your pupils' writing in some detail, what features seem to jump out at you? One way of thinking about this is to use categories that roughly correspond to the National Literacy Strategy:

1   Word level.

2   Sentence level.

3   Text level.

- How do you think your pupils are doing at Word level (on their spelling and punctuation)? Room for improvement?

- How do you think they are doing at Sentence level (in their 'style' – their grammar and sentence construction)? Could do better?

- What about at Text level (their 'Purpose and Organization', the structure of their piece), which in SATs carries three times as many marks as the other two categories?

Very often the Text area is actually the weakest of them all. Are you surprised by that? (See our action research in the CPR Success Zone, page 16; www.bravetales.com for example.)

What I am saying is that you pick up a piece of writing and think: 'Oh, my dear life, this kid can't spell or use full stops!'

And: 'Oh, my dear life, this kid can't put a proper sentence together!'

But, these two surface features are masking a much deeper, more drastic problem: 'This kid has no idea what constitutes a story!'

You and I have probably got a fairly good handle on 'Story'. We instinctively know that we have to:

1   Set up a character (or characters).
2   Make them go through some sort of crisis/process.
3   Resolve loose threads to make a neat ending.

Can we assume that the same is true about our pupils?

How many plots do you know by heart? Meaning could you stumble through the sequence of events and just about get the whole story explained. Ask your class how many stories they know in this way. The answer may be disappointingly small (or it may be refreshingly large).

It is, in fact, very useful to have a class 'plot bank' – the more stories we know well, the more plot lines we have to draw upon when creating new stories.

There is a school of thought that says it is impossible to create a genuinely new story as there are only seven possible plots (Booker, 2004). The implications of this are quite profound and we'll explore them later.

But, back to your pupils. Maybe they were not reared on a diet of fairytales. Maybe no one read Beatrix Potter or Narnia to them. Maybe they've spent most of their life rooted in front of the TV and computer screen with their plethora of characters and settings but precious little in the way of plot.

So, how can we make up for this deficit? Tactic number one is simply to tell stories. Tactic numbers two and three are probably to tell stories too. All human beings love a story. The more frequently young people hear a story, the more they build up their own plot bank and the more plot options they have to tell themselves. With more options on constructing internal narratives about their own life story, the wiser they become. Oh yes, and their own story writing improves drastically too.

But you do need to get a bit more deliberate and proactive here. You require pupils to understand what constitutes a plot and to grasp how a story structure works. The first tool that many people clutch at is to 'bullet point' the plot. Now for those who are literate, competent readers, bullet points may well offer a succinct summary of events.

But aren't you dealing with a class, at least half of whom you would never describe as literate, competent readers?

I *told* them I couldn't read and write back in Reception class but they still keep on asking me!

To these children, bullet points are often just another layer of obstacles between themselves and the actual task. Far from being helpful, bullet points have a function roughly similar to rolls of barbed wire along the top of an already impenetrable fence! If you are a bullet point user, don't groan and despair. Bullet points are a powerful tool if you are very careful about how you set them up (more on that later, see page 104).

So, the single, all-powerful, problem-solving, answer-to-all-evils, the tool that enables children to conceive of, understand and plan coherent plots, the accessible, instantly understandable, user-friendly magic wand is ... THE STORYBOARD!

▶ What are storyboards?

Working as a storyteller, people often say to me: How do you remember all those stories? Meaning: 'That's an awful lot of words!'

I tell them that I don't remember the words. I remember the pictures! I see each story as a sequence of pictures. So, the storytelling experience could be described as shown below.

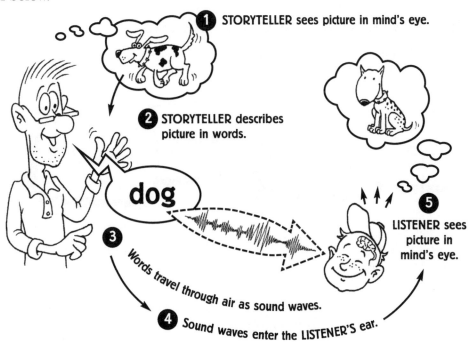

● The storytelling process

A storyboard is just a sequence of pictures that depicts a plot (think Raymond Brigg's *Father Christmas*, think *Beano*!). But, there are a few hints and tips that increase the usefulness and power of storyboards as a tool.

How many pictures?

Children usually instantly understand when you say that you are going to tell the story in pictures. Try asking them how many pictures will be needed ... 24? ... 72? ... 365? ... 9,281,648? ... Lots!

The problem with 'lots' is – how do you know how far to nudge the action forward for each scene? With an unlimited number of scenes, pupils tend to move the action forward in minuscule stages and, very often, fail to complete the whole story.

Also, with 8 or 16, or 32, or however many scenes, what do you call each scene? Scene Number 1, Scene Number 2 and so on? That's not going to necessarily help us conceive the structure. We need help in understanding what is different about each stage of the story, not just an arbitrary sequence of moments.

So, here's the challenge: we are going to tell the story in only...

For very little people (Foundation, Year 1, perhaps Year 2) the answer is three pictures. These three are our well-known friends: Beginning, Middle and End. Dealing with three chunks of story is a massive step forward from just 'draw a picture and write about it'. One picture is an event; three pictures are a plot (however rudimentary).

Before long, you can progress to scenes that have an even more purposeful description. In most instances, you may find it easiest to use four scene storyboards. Not least because it is easier to divide your sheet of paper that way!

What are these story stages called?

Try giving pairs of pupils flashcards with these words on them and see if they can get them in the right order.

It is worthwhile exploring each of these terms a little to build understanding; ask pupils what each word means.

Introduction   Far more than just a beginning, this word has connotations of a meeting. We need to say 'hello' to the main character(s) and be given an idea of the setting, that is, the world in which the story will take place.

Build-up   Can you suggest a better term than this rather vague description? Here is where you need to lay your 'hooks', set the seeds that are essential for the later action to make sense.

Climax   Some people use the terms 'problem', 'dilemma' or 'conflict'. 'Climax' can include any of these terms. You can translate the word as meaning 'the most exciting bit'. Every story needs some kind of crisis!

Resolution   Far more than just an ending, this word has connotations of solving or sorting things out. We need to tie up any loose threads and (probably) return to some sort of status quo.

So, if we put them all together we get:

1 Introduction	**2** Build-up
3 Climax	**4** Resolution

Now, we do not need to be wedded irretrievably to four scenes and there are, in fact, many good reasons for choosing five. Many mnemonics rely on that 'handy' number. Pie Corbett advocates a five-scene structure (Corbett, 2001: 19) and Booker analyses each of the seven basic plots into a five-stage format (Booker, 2004). The main hesitation in using five is simply the difficulty pupils have in dividing up the page into five boxes!

If you do wish to use five scenes, probably the best five-shape goes:

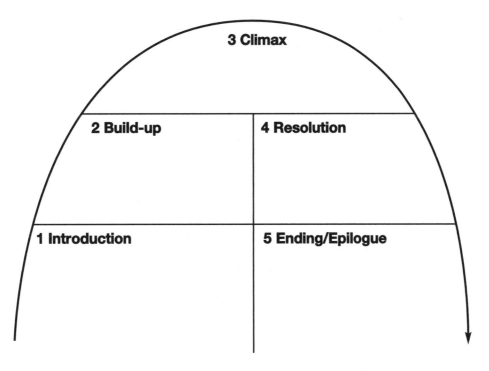

● The Story Mountain (after Pie Corbett)

This can be used successfully with even very young children, although they obviously need the template drawn for them.

▶ Creating storyboards

Visualizing

Let's begin at the beginning.

Which picture can you see in your head for the introduction of the story *Little Red Riding Hood*?

Close your eyes...
Insert a finger in your left ear...
Just inside, at the back, there's a little switch.
Click it down and switch on your in-head...
wide-screen...
technicolour...
personalized...
visualization projector!

- Which characters do we need to meet at the beginning of the story? How are they feeling? Can you see the expressions on the characters' faces?

- Are there any other details that give a clue to the characters' profession, gender, age, cultural background, attitude?

- What about the setting?

  - How far away can you see your picture?

  - What's on the horizon?

  - What about close-up?

  - What's underfoot/nearby?

Questions such as these are rhetorical. They do not require verbal responses but they help prompt the visualizing process. Like all skills, some of us are better at visualizing than others. Some people say that when they close their eyes, it's just black!

I can't do it.

Many people find maths difficult (or music or artwork and so on) but we still expect them to have a go, practise, develop, get better, LEARN! Lots of people find it hard at first, but it's amazing how quickly you get good at it with a bit of practice. Try visualizing just the sea to start with.

Visualizing is a crucially important life skill. How can you build the biggest greenhouses on the planet unless you can see them superimposed on that old clay pit (and communicate your vision to others)? How can we improve our own life unless we can see ourselves achieving our goals? In fact, how are we going to make the world a better place in any way unless we see possible solutions and envisage positive outcomes?

So, you've got a class full of pupils all visualizing 'seeing' the introduction to the story. How will you get at/make use of these images? You could try climbing inside each person's ear and clambering about to find their in-head projector (not recommended). Or, you could ask everyone to reveal their visualization through drawing.

Once again, there are possible obstacles:

This bit of negative self-talk doesn't usually kick in until we're about nine or ten years old and we go through the 'my drawing of a dog doesn't actually look like a real dog' crisis (for a brilliant book on the subject, see *The New Drawing on the Right Side of the Brain* by Betty Edwards (2001)).

Get around these obstacles by using A4 whiteboards – everyone can scrawl away in the safety of the group and then wipe it off leaving no record of their incompetence! Also, by using one whiteboard between two and taking it in turns to 'describe' and 'draw', we can practise important speaking and listening skills at the same time (see page 52).

What is very rewarding is the peace and tranquillity that settles on a class as everyone goes into their own little world of imagination. But, never let them have too long.

● Paired drawings

One complaint I have had from teachers trying out storyboarding is: 'They get all finickety and precious, spending *ages* on each picture and never complete their storyboard!'

Simple – just say: 'You have *two* minutes only to complete your picture of the introduction… one minute … 30 seconds …10 seconds until tops on pens … 10, 9, 8, 7, 6, 5, 4, 3, 2, 1 … tops on pens! … Now show me your pen with its top on!' We now have an opportunity, as so often through the school day, to focus on one person's offering, 'spotlighting' their effort in praise or damnation before 'everyone who matters in their little world'.

So, rather than single out one person's picture, concentrate on specific content, such as: 'I can see a lot of cottages. Hold your board up if you've drawn the little cottage in the woods.'

Another positive aspect of using whiteboards (and about storytelling generally) is that everyone is allowed to have their own personal version of the pictures. The variation across a group of offerings is a wonderful thing – be sure to celebrate the diversity of images.

Collect pupils' contributions and transfer them to your whole-class storyboard at the front; for example, draw a little cottage with hybrid features from several pupils' drawings. Or, get pupils to come forward and contribute an item to the 'collaborative drawing'.

There's a chance for some positive reinforcement for needier members of the group. For example, if someone who is not confident has drawn a clear facial expression on their matchstick man, concentrate on that detail: 'Whose drawings show me how Little Red was feeling? Oh look, here's a wonderful excited expression on Nathan's picture.'

Keep collecting ideas and adding them to the whole-class storyboard until your introduction picture is nearly complete. Then ask something like:

 Have you got anything *important* in your picture, which I have left out of mine?

You forgot to draw the basket!

I've drawn some flowers!

The basket! Does the story 'work' without the basket? No? The basket is an important part of the plot.

Flowers might be just the right atmospheric detail you need, but be careful – is it actually *important* to have flowers?

Pupils may choose whether or not to include atmospheric details in their picture. But make it clear that if it's in their picture, then it has to be in their story.

At this point, we finalize on an agreed class version of the first picture of our storyboard (the 'Introduction').

Apocryphal story

One teaching assistant came on a course with me and, all fired-up, suggested storyboarding to her Year 3 and 4 class teacher (who was struggling desperately to engage and motivate a determinedly non-literate class). The class teacher replied: 'That would be going back to Key Stage 1 work – they are juniors now!'

It transpired that, with Ofsted just around the corner, she was terrified of being caught out with her class drawing pictures when they should be writing!

If only she'd known that just down the road another teacher was brave enough to use storyboarding during the inspection and was told by the Inspector: 'Great! Real Text level work – no words or sentences to get in the way!'

Next step

What shall we do next? Wipe our boards clean and move on to draw the Build-up?

NO!

If we move on to draw the next picture, how far forward do we progress the story? Pupils tend to move it a tiny bit, then another tiny bit and, once again we've used up 17 squares before we've got to the Climax! No, the challenge is to do this thing in four (or three or five) scenes.

So, we will jump to the ending next and visualize the final scene. With many stories it is relevant to phrase the challenge thus: 'What are the fewest number of changes you can make to your Introduction picture to change it into a Resolution (or Ending) picture?'

If you are working on an interactive whiteboard, just copy and paste the first picture into the final box, then ask individual pupils to come out and make minor alterations. Often, the final picture has many elements in common with the initial picture, for example:

Introduction

Resolution

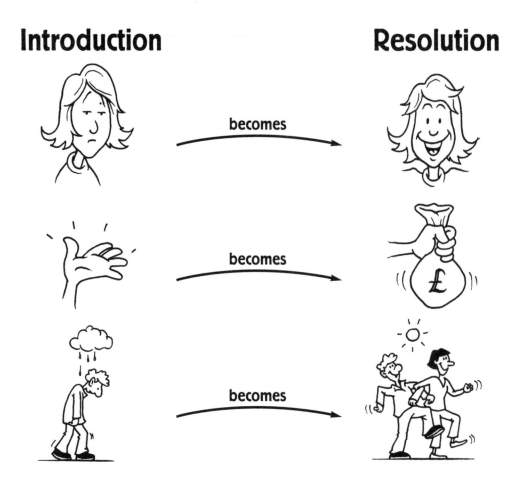

becomes

becomes

becomes

● Transforming beginnings into endings

Climax

With the 'pedn ha teen' (top and tail) complete, we can turn our attention to the body of the story. Working backwards, it's usually easy to identify the Climax of the story – normally the most memorable moment. If there's blood and gore, that's probably it. It's often the incident that children would instinctively pick to draw. When I was at school (Jurassic Infants), after being read a story, we were unfailingly asked to 'write about it and draw a picture' (in that order too – no, you can't draw your picture until you've finished your writing!). We probably all drew the Climax. I wish they had asked us to draw three pictures (Beginning, Middle and End) first and then write a sentence for each picture.

Because the Climax features so large in our memory of any given story, young people often forget to go past it! When you ask for the Ending, you get given the Climax. The woodcutter never gets to come barging in and Little Red Riding Hood is left suspended forever with 'All the better to eat you with!' ringing in her ears as the Wolf devours her. Tom kills the giant (bloodily) but they forget to marry him off to the heroine. Lutey will escape the Mermaid's clutches but they forget to give him his magic comb and attitude transplant.

Storyboarding solves that problem in a flash – as we usually put the ending in before we have dealt with the Climax.

Some stories do have messy or multiple Climax scenes and, on occasions, you may be forced to sub-divide them, but you need a very good reason to do so.

● Storyboard for *Tommy Trevorrow* with double climax

● Storyboard for *Jooan Choy* with triple climax

Remember, storyboarding is a tool to aid simplification – we can get rid of surplus, unnecessary incidents or characters.

Build-up

Working backwards again, the Build-up becomes self-explanatory: 'What has to have happened earlier so that the Climax makes sense?'

And before you know it you have a completed storyboard!

● Storyboard for Little Red

Adding (written) speech bubbles is one of the obvious ways of developing the storyboard further.

● Example completed Little Red storyboard with speech bubbles

Having created a large whole-class storyboard, you might want to allow everyone to draw their own A4 versions. If you have done the collaborative storyboard on an interactive whiteboard, you can just print everyone out a copy.

The first time you create storyboards as a class, you probably need to go through the whole step-by-step process. It's worth it, honest – pupils' understanding of Story develops in leaps and bounds. But, subsequently, once everyone has got the hang of it, it is not necessary to do the whole process. For instance, offer pupils a storyboard with Introduction and Resolution already complete (after all, they are the easy bits) and get them to work out the Climax and Build-up. Or draw the entire storyboard but leave out a vital character, ask pupils to track that character's journey through the story and draw them in.

What's next?

Write the story?

Well, we could and the written outcomes' versions will be immensely improved just by having developed our understanding of the plot. But, if you can hold off the desperate pressure to make them write for just a while longer, then there's a lot more productive, worthwhile fun to be had yet.

Please, please, whatever you do, get the children retelling the story before you ask them to write (see pages 36, 62 and 85 for guidance).

▶ The uses of storyboards

Storyboards are the solution to just about all problems known to Teacherland! The potential and possibilities are enormous.

However, here are the three main uses that we can put storyboarding to.

1 *Plot analysis.* As in the process described above, it is quite simply the easiest and most powerful tool to encourage a good grasp of plot components. It can be used to analyse fairytales, whole novels, entire epics or single scenes. Don't believe me? Look at these examples.

● *Lord of the Rings* storyboard

● *Macbeth* storyboard

2 *Preparation and support for telling.* Whenever you are preparing to tell a new story, always begin by storyboarding it. This helps you to understand the most important elements and structure of the plot. The storyboard then becomes your safety net, your prompt sheet. Show your scribbles to your audience or class and say: 'Here's my storyboard, if I get stuck or go wrong I'll look at the pictures to remind me.'

In fact, once you've *drawn* the pictures, your visual memory clicks in and it's amazing how well you remember them. If you do get lost, you can glance at your storyboard and remind yourself instantly. If you were glancing down at a piece of prose text, you would take ages to find your place and then get sucked back into 'reading' rather than 'telling'.

3 *Creating new story.* So far, the whole book has been about retelling known stories. That is deliberate. Walk before you run. However, later on we will be looking at approaches to creating new story, and storyboards will figure largely (see page 37).

Retelling from your storyboard

The first important, major function of the storyboard is to provide an instant, easy-to-use crib sheet to support us in our retelling of the story. With a storyboard to help you, retelling becomes easily achievable (and even enjoyable!). Work with one scene at a time (eating a whole elephant in one go is a bit of a jumbo task). Simply point to each object, character or item in the current picture, include it in your narrative and you can be confident that the plot will 'hang together'.

The first time you retell from the storyboard you may like to do it 'badly on purpose', mumbling in a very inexpressive way: 'There was this little girl and she lived in this little cottage in the woods and her Mum wanted her to take a basket of stuff to her Granny.'

Pupils can then pick you up and refer you back to the success criteria chart 'What do Good Storytellers do?', which you have previously created and displayed (see page 10).

Ah ha, so you'd like me use FACIAL EXPRESSIONS? Everybody, show me a facial expression that I might use?

You want me to include GESTURE? Where in this picture is there a chance to use some good gesture? Demonstrate for me!

You want me to use DIRECT SPEECH? What do you think Little Red might say? After three, all together, let's hear Little Red speaking, one, two, three.

Encouraging the pupils to teach you how to do it properly is a good teaching strategy across the majority of classroom situations. It keeps everyone engaged. It also gives them safe 'rehearsal' opportunities in advance of their doing it for themselves.

You might like to demonstrate how, within the scene, you can point to the objects in an entirely different order and the scene still works. Or, you might like to retell and deliberately 'forget' to point to a key item (for example, the basket) and see if the class pick you up.

Eventually, model retelling successfully – including all the 'good' techniques from the chart. (We will explore 'Choose good words' in greater depth on page 62).

Use 'Listening partners' to get pupils retelling scenes from the story to each other orally/aurally. Don't know exactly what is meant by 'Listening partners'? There's a whole section on the subject coming up (see page 52).

▶ Transforming stories

Write a story; it can be about anything you like!

What a nightmare brief! Most people's brains go into shut down (see page 77) with too many possibilities (and opportunities to foul-up) crowding in. We do try to help a little by invoking a planning process. This usually means we make notes or bullet points covering the characters, the setting and the plot.

Character Most pupils can just about manage to create character – there's always a new swathe of characters coming at you on the telly or just name all your mates.

Setting Again, not too tough, somewhere from your daily experience, school, supermarket or even a fantasy 'dark woods' or 'North Pole' are not too hard to imagine.

Plot Oh dear – we've got at least two problems now:

1 Most children are only just beginning to grasp what is meant by or what constitutes plot; how can they create a sensible new story structure?

2 As militant non-writers, many pupils see the bullet point planning process as another obstacle, an interim grim task to be got through before the main grim task.

The truth is that to come up with a new plot is actually very difficult. You and I might be able to do it. With our lifetimes' experiences of story, we have a pretty good idea how to shape events to make a plot. Children don't (yet). They still need the experience of exploring plot to begin to establish a feel for what makes a story. Which is why, until they are really confident, I say: 'Don't make up a new plot. Pinch one from somewhere else!'

To be really sure of success, first of all we copy, then we *adapt* and, *finally*, we *create from scratch*. As Pie Corbett says, the process goes: 'Imitate … Innovate … Invent.'

There is no such thing as 'art in a vacuum' – all creative ventures are inspired by and based upon previous work. No one complained that *West Side Story* was 'lifted' from Shakespeare's *Romeo and Juliet* – people thought Bernstein was inspired! Of course, Shakespeare himself didn't make up that story either but 'lifted' it from several earlier sources. If you agree with Booker (2004) that there are only seven basic plots, then you should feel even less guilty – they've all been done before!

I discovered this idea accidentally and rather furtively when panicking to complete a GCSE English Language essay. Stuck for ideas, I merely rewrote the Isaac Asimov story I had just been reading, in my own words with new characters and setting. Result? A+!

Without letting on to teachers or peers, I adopted this success formula and guaranteed myself A grades right through.

Now, looking back, I think: 'What was the *guilt* for? Our teacher should have taught us how to pinch plot and structure from elsewhere!'

We can call this process *story transformation*. And it starts, as easy as pie, for beginners and little people with a Beginning, Middle and End of a story we know and love.

● 'Little Red' template storyboard showing a Beginning, Middle and End

Story transformation at KS1

To minimize confusion, we are going to keep both the main character and the plot the same. You are merely going to change the setting and the supporting characters. Ask the class: 'What would happen if, *instead* of going into the woods, Little Red Riding Hood went … underwater?'

You can model this process by colour-coding each character or object in the template storyboard, then asking the class to suggest how we might change each item in our new storyboard (keeping the colour the same to emphasize correspondence).

Be quite strict about the transforming; if something exists in the template picture, it must be transposed (and/or transformed) into the new storyboard.

● 'Little Red' transformed storyboard

Everyone instantly 'gets' the pattern of the new story and pupils begin to understand that a plot exists independently from the characters and setting that are usually associated with it.

Retelling these transformed stories is great fun, there are lots of opportunity for collaboration, joining in repeated phrases and so on – 'What big fins you've got!'

Two common venues for KS1 transformations are 'Underwater' and 'Outer space' – two locations that give you plenty of scope for fantasy and invention, and minimize the chances of anachronisms, incongruities or mistakes.

Story transformation at KS2

When transforming with older pupils, you can push the process in various ways. You can change the main character as well as the supporting cast and the setting.

Are your pupils struggling with a particular genre (be it science fiction, fantasy or whatever)? Taking the plot of a well-known fairytale (which are usually of a neat manageable structure) and transforming it into the target genre is a good way to ensure concentration on the features of the target genre, knowing that the plot is taken care of.

● Modern retelling of *Cinderella*

● Dickensian retelling of *Three Little Pigs*

● Science fiction version of Little Red

As well as helping us to understand about different genres, this exercise can also reinforce content from other areas of the curriculum (history, geography, RE).

It also begins to bring to light the archetypal structure of stories. Once freed from the specific cultural details that the story was received with, when translated to an alternative cultural setting, the basic human similarities are what stands out.

Later in this book, we will model a similar story transformation that uses bullet points and is even more fool-proof than this process (see page 112)!

Sam's journey

Sam was a Year 4 SEN pupil whose class had been studying traditional tales for two weeks in preparation for writing a modern retelling. Unfortunately, at no point had anyone actually told a story – Sam found the whole thing boring as usual.

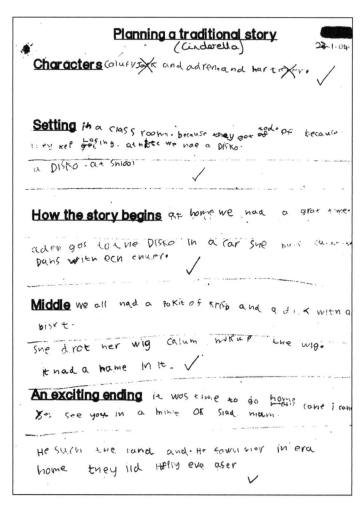

● Sam's bullet point plan – note slip into present tense narrative

● Sam's poor first attempt at writing –
moderated as a level 1A

Yet just one short week later Sam produced this:

● Sam's transformed story –
moderated as a level 2C

How was this startling change brought about? Simple.

- The teaching assistant, Margaret Porter, asked if she could take the SEN group for a week.

- She told them a story (*Three Billy Goats Gruff*).

- They storyboarded the plot and then the pupils retold the story.

- They transformed the storyboard and told their new versions to each other.

- Sam had his transformed storyboard with him (instead of the bullet point plan) during the unaided writing task.

Not rocket science, just good practice!

Chapter **3**

Speaking and listening

▶ What do good listeners do?

I've often heard an exasperated teacher cry: 'But they just don't know how to listen!'

Probably true, but if pupils do not know how to do something, isn't it, as teachers, our job to teach them how to do it? Let's teach our young people to be good listeners. As with most teaching, a good place to start is by finding out what they already know, or what their current attitude is, or what they understand so far.

Try asking your class this question: 'What is the difference between "listening" and "hearing"?'

One way of answering this question is by asking everyone to close their eyes and count on their fingers how many different sounds they can hear. You might ask them to listen to the traffic noise, or birdsong or the heater's hum. Many sounds are perfectly audible when we concentrate and listen to them. Actually, we could hear them all along but were not paying them any attention.

So listening implies a certain focus, concentration or attention.

Listening games

Ask everyone to close their eyes. Move about the room and find three (or more) ways to make a sound. For example:

- 'Here comes sound number 1 ...' (rattle pens in a pot)
- 'Here comes sound number 2 ...' (click electricity switch on and off)
- 'Here comes sound number 3 ...' (crumple paper in the waste bin)

Now pupils can put their hands up and guess. But don't just tell them if they're right or wrong. Follow their suggestions (for example, rattle scissors in the tray) and see if they can tell if it is right or wrong.

This sort of teaching can be developed into other discrimination games. Perhaps, using a screen and identical sets of 'noise-makers' in front and behind. Pupils come forward to try to replicate the target noise that someone has made behind the screen. Before long you are into developing real musical discrimination as pupils copy sound patterns or even sequences of pitched notes.

I'll often say to individuals in a class: 'Thank you for listening to me' or 'I can tell you are a good listener'. How do I know when someone's really listening to me? In other words,

What do GOOD LISTENERS do?

Even very young children will begin to come up with suggestions such as:

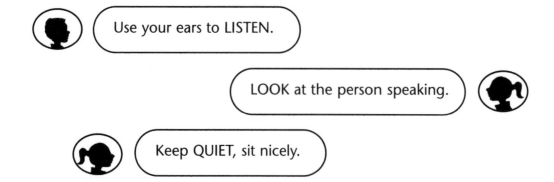

Use your ears to LISTEN.

LOOK at the person speaking.

Keep QUIET, sit nicely.

Older pupils might add further ideas:

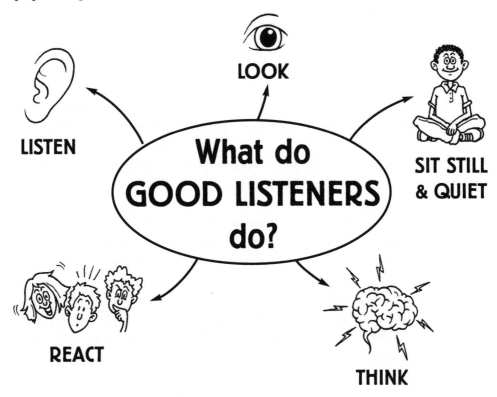

This is another success criteria chart. Every child deserves to experience success every day! So the clearer we can be about the desired behaviour or outcome, the easier it is to let them know when they get it right.

Make a display chart of this diagram (or similar) and put it up on the classroom wall. Keep it colourful, visual and easy to interpret (how many children in your class have difficulty accessing information displayed as writing?).

If you want to really make an impact on listening behaviour, explore your chart a little further:

LISTEN   Play around with listening games but impose certain rules such as 'cover both ears with your hands' or 'cup your ears'. Try making cardboard 'elephant ears' that you hold behind your own ear – it does make an amazing difference to sounds.

LOOK   Of course it is possible to be listening intently while not looking. Shutting out visual distraction can even help sometimes. But, in terms of communicating via speech, visual information can be very important. Try whispering to the class with their eyes shut, and then repeat with their eyes open – they are better lip-readers than they thought! Sit pairs back-to-back to whisper top secret messages – see how difficult that is compared with face to face?

SIT STILL & QUIET Ask the class to fidget and grumble or, depending how brave you are, leap about and sing. Give them several pieces of information while they are moving. Some will instantly calm down and become quiet and still. Those who continue to move and make a noise will not get the information.

THINK Listening needs to be an active activity, not just some passive absence of activity. So giving listeners a task to think about pulls their focus and concentration. This could be as simple as: 'Listen out for three words beginning with B in this passage' or 'Find out what your partner liked the most.'

REACT Older children can understand that we are not entirely inert when we listen to someone speaking. Have you ever been interviewed by local TV? They turn the camera on the interviewer to do the 'noddies'. He stands there alone, nodding and smiling like an insane chimpanzee so that they can chip in short snips of him nodding as if 'reacting'. Get your class to practise giving 'noddies'. Pantomime it up at first. You can call it 'supporting the speaker' – little nods, smiles, eyebrow-lifts all make us feel that we are being listened to.

LISTENING MANTRA With very little people, for whom even a colourful chart on the wall is rather distant and complex, devise a 'listening mantra'. This is just a short sequence of actions with words that you practise, learn by heart, and then repeat every time you need some good listening to happen. For example, teacher asks: 'What do good listeners do?' Everyone chants back: 'They LISTEN, they LOOK, they SIT STILL and KEEP QUIET.'

It is always better to personalize these charts to gain a sense of ownership, so make up your own class version!

It can be very effective to join together a speaking success chart with a listening success chart. This will come in very useful for defining clear roles when using listening partners (see page 52).

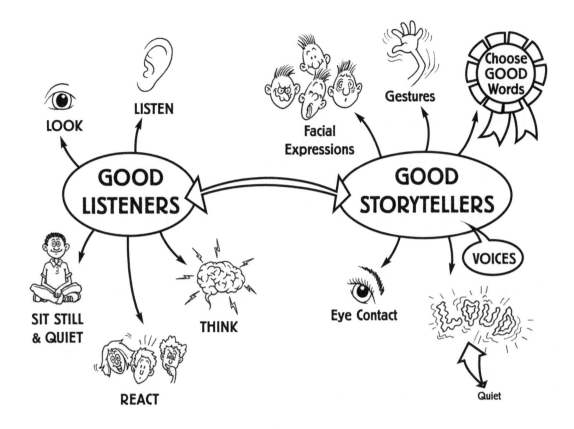

▶ Speaking and listening

If we imagine the lines of communication in a traditional classroom, we might imagine the teacher communicating along 30 or so spokes of a wheel.

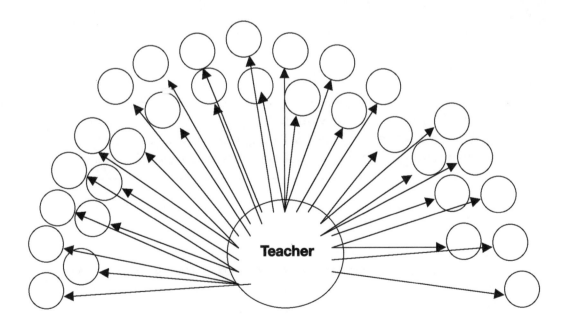

● Teacher attempting to communicate with 30 individuals

The teacher is the main focus and is 'on stage' a lot of the time. In the above model, how much personal attention or one-to-one feedback might any one pupil expect to get? Approximately one-thirtieth of the teacher's time, perhaps? Teacher attention is often very lop-sided and perhaps 15 per cent of the pupils receive 85 per cent of the attention. Some pupils can expect to receive no teacher attention in the classroom at all unless it is of the behaviour management type – 'Sit down, shut-up; do as you are told!' This is the reason for some cynicism about the phenomenon known as 'class discussion'. What that often means in practice is that the teacher interacts with a small handful of keen, interested pupils, while the majority switch off, daydream or, at best, passively attend. So, it is essential that we break up this pattern of communication and make fuller use of the other human beings in the room.

There is another issue here as well: teachers may set up speaking and listening opportunities. These might include, for instance, sharing news, show and tell, or class discussions.

My challenge to this is: these may be times that pupils can practise speaking and listening, but how many such occasions are structured opportunities to learn how to get better at speaking and listening?

Skilful use of questioning is one of the most effective implements in the teacher's cutlery drawer of techniques. We all know the difference between open and closed questioning and which it might be appropriate to use when. But, even so, question-and-answer sessions can easily become a grim experience for all involved.

Here's the scenario of a well-meaning teacher asking an open-ended question.

 Who's got a good idea for the main character for our story?

Maybe a half-a-dozen hands shoot up.

(*thinks*) Hum, it's always the same few ... Better not choose Charlotte again ... There's Sally day dreaming as usual, not even paying attention, I'll pull her back to attention ... Sally?

Silence ... Sally looks awkward.

Can you give us a good idea for a main character for our story Sally?

Silence ...other children turn to look at Sally.

Come on!

Silence … the classroom ceiling opens, a huge, bright spotlight beams down, fixing Sally into rigid fear. All the eyes (of everyone who matters in the world) are fixed upon her.

> Come on Sally … it could be anything! (*thinks*) The girl has gone into rigor mortis! Blinking heck, it's not as if it's a difficult question; she clearly has no imagination!

The 'spotlight scenario' is played out many, many times in many, many classrooms – not always leading to a massive show down but almost inevitably leading to some sense of failure for the pupil. Build up a sequence of such experiences on a daily basis and young people spiral down into self-deprecating inertia.

We often ask pupils to do what appear to be simple tasks but which really require more than one skill to accomplish. Very often teaching is about breaking down some final task into manageable bits and their reassembling it in achievable steps.

Even when asking something as simple as an open-ended question we are often expecting children to do at least two things at once:

1 Be creative! *Here, now,* come up with a *good* idea!

2 Share your idea publicly! Bring your effort into the open to be judged by all of us!

The combination of these two pressures leads to clam-up. Extra pressure just creates a tighter clam.

So are your pupils actually lacking in imagination? Do you have a room full of non-creative souls? Probably not (see Chapter 4).

The greatest resource in any classroom is the students themselves.

In the classroom below, each pupil has a great deal more opportunity to communicate along a variety of channels.

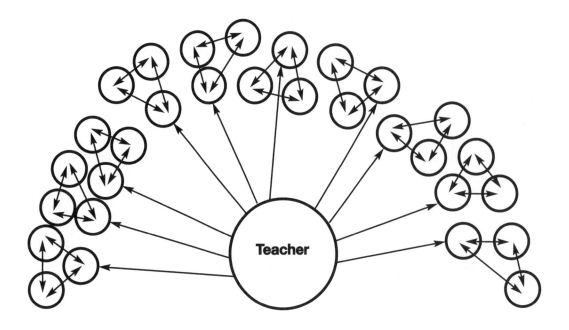

● Teacher communicating with ten groupings, each individual
receiving more than one line of communication

It is easy to draw such a theoretical diagram but, in reality, how do we ensure that appropriate and constructive communication is taking place along pupil–pupil channels?

In an adult situation, we probably would not hesitate to say: 'Turn to the person next to you and have a chat about that.' This request assumes that everyone present is sufficiently mature and well socialized to be able to:

- locate the person next to them;
- overcome shyness or cultural obstacles;
- shut up now and again and let the other person get a word in edgeways!

We cannot make these assumptions with children (especially young children) and we probably need to lead them through a sequence of activity to make it very clear what the roles and responsibilities are.

▶ Listening partners

Some people call them 'work buddies' or 'response partners', but 'listening partners' just keeps the emphasis on the active listening component. Scarcely a moment of the school day goes by when some sort of listening partner activity would not be relevant.

If you have ever endured the agony of little Emily attempting to share her news with the whole class (a class that would rather fidget and poke each other than attend to Emily's self-conscious mumblings), then you will probably be delighted to share news with listening partners. Everyone gets a bit of gossiping done and, having rehearsed in safety, any contributions selected for public sharing are far slicker.

But at any moment of decision, prediction, survey or practice, engage the whole class by asking them to turn to their partners and,

- predict what will happen next in the story;
- find out what variety of pets everyone has;
- suggest a good way of testing the strength of the materials;
- turn this into a complex sentence.

Step-by-step listening partners made easy

Finding a partner

Getting into pairs needs to be as quick and fuss-free as possible. If you are working with the whole class sitting on the carpet area, then just ask everyone to turn, without talking, and face the person sitting next to them. Instruct everyone to remain silent but anyone without a partner should put their hand up. It's then simple to join up stranded solos to form pairs. If there is an odd number in the class, the remaining child can work with you or another adult or form a threesome. (Always ask teaching assistants or other adults present to join in at precisely the same level as the pupils. Very often modelling appropriate pupil behaviour is the most effective thing a support worker can do.)

It needn't take long to join-up pupils if you are keen to get mixed-ability pairings. Just rattle out pairs of names from the top and bottom of your ability spectrum and let them find each other.

One Key Stage 1 teacher of my acquaintance has a book of carpet sample squares and each child knows and loves their own colourful patch. Just before the pupils come in, she scatters the carpet squares, rigging it so that undesirables are kept apart and needy pupils are next to a supportive partner.

If working at desks, then partner choice is somewhat predetermined by the seating plan. The seating plan itself can be organized to ring the changes, or pupils can be trained to 'walk and talk'.

The 'walk and talk' instruction is to leave your desk and find your partner (previously allocated by rota), interact standing up and then return to your desk. (Perhaps it could be called 'walk and listen', 'go and hear' or 'rendezvous and receive'?)

Do you give pupils some choice about whom they will work with? Can you, at the same time, explicitly challenge them to push back the frontiers of their comfort zone by choosing to work with an unfamiliar partner?

True story

One Year 6 class I was working with had a big problem over working with the opposite gender. Boys and girls were two very different camps and a lot of niggles and teasing was the norm. I decided to bring this into the open.

> Think about someone in the class who you are used to working with, who you feel safe working with…
> Now think of someone (no looking, or pointing) you would not feel comfortable with; the person you would *least* like to work with…
> Everyone in the class must fit somewhere along a line between these two extremes.
> The challenge is this: 'How far along the line can you go? Who will you work with next to extend your own comfort zone!'

Off they went to find partners – theoretically each would now be able to make their own choice about how 'dangerously' they would live.

One rather socially dependent boy found himself partnered by one of the socially dominant boys and, thinking he could score a few points, whispered in an unpleasant snigger: 'Look! John's working with Sophie!'

I felt my hackles rise and was about to come back with some sarcastic comment (always a mistake) such as: 'Do you know, yesterday I was working with a class where a boy was partnered with a girl and at the end of the session … he was still a boy! What's more, they didn't even have to get married or anything!' But, saving me from having to make such an unworthy response, the socially dominant boy replied: 'John's working with Sophie? That's nothing! I'm going to work with *Amy*!'

And off he went.

The unsaid implication being that he was even more macho than John because Amy was even 'further out' than Sophie!

Through short, sharp activities, plenty of quick-fire partner changes and structured positive feedback we really turned the culture around in that class until everyone was used to working with everyone else.

Who's listening?

Who's going to be listening? Another opportunity for more fuss and bother as pairs argue about who will listen or speak first. You could try something like:

> No speaking, using only eyes and facial expression, make a decision between the two of you. One of you will keep your hands in your lap. One of you will put a hand up.

The idea here is to trick them into eye contact and non-verbal communication. Then it's simple: 'Well done, those with their hands up have the hardest job first because they are going to show us just what good listeners they are! Remember … what do good listeners do?'

Revisit your Good listeners success criteria chart on the wall or re-run your listening mantra to make it crystal clear what is expected of listeners. In particular, make sure listeners are clear what they are supposed to be THINKING about. Tell them what question to expect when they have completed their listening. For example:

- 'After you've listened, Listeners, I am going to ask you: *What did your partner get for Christmas?*' (news)

- 'After you've listened, Listeners, I am going to ask you: *What does your partner predict will happen next?*' (science, literacy)

- 'After you've listened, Listeners, I am going to ask you: *What choice of atmospheric language did your partner use in their storytelling?*'

Who's speaking?

Notice that because of our concentration on the listening end of the equation we have put very little emphasis on what the speaker might be talking about. This is right and proper; it actually diffuses the pressure on the speaker to come up with some marvellous (funny, original, clever and so on) contribution.

Safety of the herd

Another way to help speakers overcome any initial difficulties is to provide them with an *en masse* rehearsal. This is a simple way to circumnavigate the fearsome pressure of the spotlight that shines on individual pupils when you ask them to contribute verbally.

Simply, ask everyone to chant the opening of a sentence together and then to carry on and finish it individually – everyone talking at once and you, as teacher, modelling a lengthy mumble over the top of the noise.

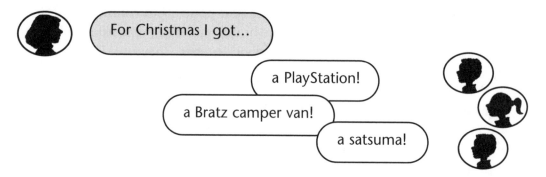

It can feel a bit strange at first but it's worth persevering as it helps generate genuinely individual responses in many contexts (instead of pupils just copying whatever the last person said because they know that that answer will be 'safe').

You can develop 'Safety of the herd' to quite a complicated extent;

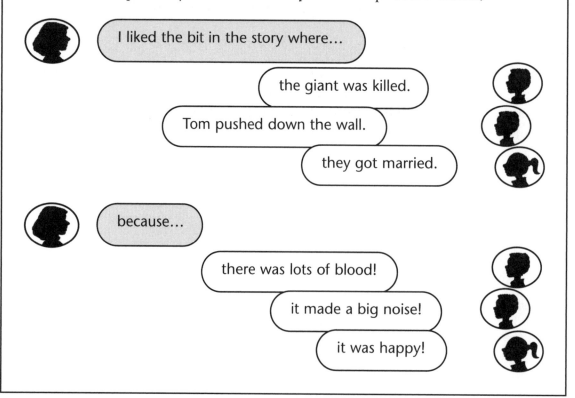

Having set up speakers with their simple task, you now need to *let go* and see what happens. *Avoid* the temptation to climb in and nudge, coach, cajole from the side.

What if a pair just sit there in silence?	Oh well, the activity is still unfamiliar, perhaps they'll get the hang of it next time (especially when they see others successful and enjoying themselves).
What if a pair are 'off task' talking about football, or discos or *EastEnders*?	Well, at least they *are* engaging in communication (remember in the old style 'class discussion' perhaps 85 per cent of the class were not properly engaged in communication at all).
Worst still, what if all pairs go off talking like mad and never shut up again? What if I lose control and have to fight to regain order?	Before they start speaking and listening, ask pairs to let you know when they have finished by turning to face you, folding arms and smiling. This gives speakers something to *do* when they have finished and prevents listeners from launching into unstructured feedback. Say 'Thank you' to each pair who turn and gaze at you – this acts as a gentle reminder to other pairs to get a move on and finish. Increase the volume of your 'Thank you!' until everyone is back looking at you.

Reporting back

It is very important to receive contributions in a structured way. You promised earlier to ask listeners a particular question, don't go moving the goalposts but stick to your original question: 'Could I have hands-up from listeners who are willing to tell us … What did your partner get for Christmas? What does your partner predict will happen next? What did your storyteller do that made the retelling enjoyable?'

Now, what can easily happen next is that one person begins to feed back and everyone else subsides back into chatter. Don't allow that to happen. If necessary, remind the whole class to once again employ their listening skills: 'Everyone, can we now please listen to Tamsyn, as she tells us what she liked about the way Jack told the story.'

It might be quite hard for Tamsyn to come up with some positive comment about Jack's storytelling, except we can refer back to our success criteria chart (see page 10) and ask Tamsyn to choose something from the chart that Jack did well. Don't allow Tamsyn to be vague and woolly; if she says she liked 'Jack's funny faces', challenge her to be very specific and describe (or demonstrate) one particular funny face.

What happens next is probably the most important moment in reporting back yet it is the moment that we frequently overlook or forget. Remember, this is a speaking and listening session with the emphasis on active improvement of listening, so it is vital that we ask something like: 'Jack, how good was Tamsyn's *listening*?'

And then press him to relate back to the success criteria chart: 'So she was *looking at you and keeping quiet*. Well done, Tamsyn, good listening. Well done, Jack, good storytelling.'

So, both Jack and Tamsyn have had some positive teacher feedback but there are 28 other little souls who have had none. Obviously, we could repeat the reporting sequence with a couple more pairs, but it would take too long to get around the whole class.

The only thing to do is to train pupils to give each other proper feedback.

▶ Feedback and coaching

Surely every child should experience success and positive feedback every day. So many youngsters receive only failure-message after failure-message; it is small wonder that their self-esteem is rock bottom.

A formula for experiencing success might go something like:

> Here are the goalposts.
> Here's how to score a goal.
> I'll help you score the first one.
> Well done; you scored!
> Now do one on your own.
> Well done; you scored again!
> (perhaps now we can begin to move the ball further back, add a goalie…)

Of course, teaching involves the professional skill and judgement of *when* to move the goalposts further away, when to add a goalkeeper and then an opposition team and so on. But, the experience of scoring goals, keeping on target, getting it *right*, is essential on a daily basis.

So, the very first stage on giving good feedback is simply to state what was good, to say what you liked, to point out success. The clearer the success criteria, the easier this becomes: 'Choose something from the GOOD LISTENERS chart that your partner did well. Now tell them, for example: *I know you were listening because you were looking at me; Thank you for giving me good 'noddies'; I liked the way you remembered exactly what I said.*'

It is not just the 'feel good factor' that results from being told what we've got right (although that is important). Often, we do not know what we are doing well until someone tells us so. Once we have been told, we can choose to do it again deliberately (instead of leaving it to chance).

Response Sandwich

Once pupils are used to the idea of giving a single bite of positive feedback, then we can train them to give constructive advice.

Once again, it deserves a chart on the wall which goes something along the lines of:

- ❤ Something I liked
- ★ Something that could improve
- ❤ Something I liked

Or

- ● It was good the way you...
- ■ Perhaps you might like to try...
- ● It was good the way you...

Or

- ✔ State a good thing
- → Suggest an improvement
- ✔ State a good thing

(Personalize! Devise your own as a class!)

For most of us our daily interactions have a large negative component: complaints, problems, blame. So it can be difficult for pupils (and adults!) to learn to phrase improvements in a *constructive* manner.

It is easy to give 'Pop Idol' style feedback, pointing out the negatives; it is far harder (and far more worthwhile) to rephrase the criticisms as a positive suggestion for improvement. Teachers need to keep modelling and making it explicit and referring back to the success criteria chart (see page 47), giving examples of constructive language. That way it is sometimes helpful to have the sentence prompt built-in. For example:

- 'Perhaps you could try...'
- 'It might be even better if you...'
- 'I'd like to see you have a go at...'

In order to avoid being negative, many of us 'nice' people tend to sidestep the middle point of the Response Sandwich: 'It was all brilliant!' 'It couldn't get any better!' Such statements are almost never true, and on some levels the recipient knows that they are getting dishonest feedback.

Put *meat* in the sandwich! Train pupils to give 'How to get better' feedback to each other.

If the Response Sandwich is working well, there are two further developments you might like to consider: coaching and meta coaching.

Coaching

In this context, this simply means embedding the Response Sandwich formula inside two powerful questions for self-evaluation. So it goes:

?	'How was that for you?'	'Well, I did all right, but I forgot to...'
❤	'I liked the way you...'	
★	'Perhaps you might try...'	
❤	'Another very strong aspect was...'	
?	'What will you do differently next time?'	'Next time I will remember to...'

This structure allows the trainee to take responsibility for their own learning, to analyse their own performance and suggest their own ways forward.

Once again, this can be used in a myriad of contexts but what might it look like in a listening lesson?

?	'How well do you think you listened?'	'Well, I was listening but I did turn around to see what Gabrielle was doing...
❤	'You were looking at me most of the time...'	
★	'I'd like it if you smiled a bit more to make me feel that you're interested in what I'm saying.'	
❤	But, you did remember the main points of what I said, so you were listening.'	
?	'What will you do differently next time you are listening?'	'I will make sure I concentrate and give you plenty of smiley "noddies"!'

Meta coaching

I know that we are in danger of going off the main point of this book again, but there is a great thing you can do with older pupils in trios.

This is just the same as coaching above but with three people.

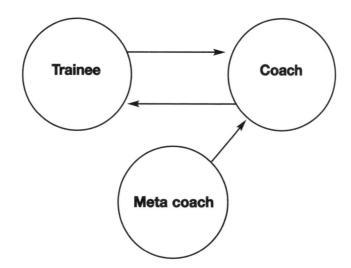

1 Trainee delivers.

2 Coach gives feedback to Trainee.

3 Meta coach gives feedback to Coach.

For example:

?	'How well do you think you coached?'	'Well, I probably didn't let her speak enough and I couldn't think of a second good thing to say.'
♥	'You did clearly tell her what she did well.'	
★	'You might try letting her talk more and plan your "good things to say" in advance.'	
♥	'I thought you were friendly and helpful in your manner.'	
?	'What will you do differently next time you are coaching?'	'I will shut up and let her speak more and save a "good thing" to finish with.'

This may sound a little brain-strangling and unfeasibly complex. But, if you get it working, it is a fabulous tool for improving the quality of feedback being given between peers.

Why should you be the only teacher in the room when you've got 30 little darlings capable of sharing your load?

▶ Chooser boards

Retelling stories

Back to the storytelling theme. The most obvious use of listening partners is to have them retelling chunks of story from the storyboard scene by scene. After each scene is told, feedback is given as described above.

We know that the children will keep to the plot because they have a storyboard to follow. So, that is the text level objectives looked after – we are working with clear purpose and organization.

But what about all those word and sentence level objectives we have to cover? Actually, listening partners is the very tool to tackle word and sentence level objectives as well – by embedding them in the retelling.

Let's start at the very beginning.

We are in Foundation or KS1. You point at the storyboard to begin retelling your story: 'Once upon a time ... hmm ... is that the best way to start my story? Are there any *other* ways to start a fairytale?'

Open questions such as these are intended to be good practice – they ought to provoke a range of suggestions from across the class. But, what if the question is outside the pupil's experience? What if most pupils do not know any other fairytale openings? What if they are too shy to speak out? What if the question is so open that they have gone into 'brain-boggle-shut-down'? (See page 77.)

Very often, the most effective action is to allow pupils to choose their responses but from a *limited* set of answers. We can provide a supported set of possible correct answers. Then, as confidence grows, the set of 'correct solutions' can be grown as well.

Let's illustrate this, still at very young people level, by displaying our first chooser board.

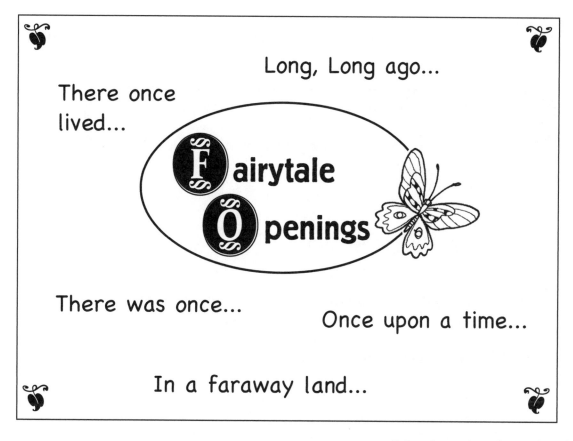

● Fairytale openings chooser board

(The butterfly in the middle is important – we'll come back to him later, see page 131.)

Now, sorry if this is teaching Granny to suck eggs, but quite a lot of these little people can't read! Simply producing some wordy chart and sticking it on the wall is not the same as training pupils how to use the thing!

So we introduce them to the chart: 'It says 'Fairytale Openings' – and all of these are different ways to start a fairytale. Billy, would you like to come out and pick one?'

Billy toddles up and points at a nice purple-coloured phrase:

That says 'Long, long ago...' Can you remember that? Shall we read it together?

Long, long ago...

Great! You help us to remember 'Long, long ago...' Billy. What about you Sam, would you like to come and choose one?

Spend a while exploring the chart and giving ownership of certain phrases to certain children. Then, when we're ready we can check for understanding through 'Safety of the herd'.

Right everybody, choose one Fairytale Opening from our chart...
After three, please whisper your chosen Fairytale Opening to me...
One, two, three...
[*everyone whispers together*]
What did you whisper Zoe?
What did you whisper Dan?

I chose 'There was once....'
So now I'm going to carry on and finish my sentence...
[*pointing at relevant picture in storyboard*]
'There was once ... a girl called Little Red Riding Hood who lived in a cottage in the middle of the woods...'

I could have chosen 'Long, long ago...'
And so I might have said...
'Long, long ago... in a little cottage in the woods there lived a girl called Little Red Riding Hood...'

How are you going to stretch your Fairytale Opening into a sentence?

After three, please whisper your 'Fairytale-Opening-stretched-into-a-sentence' to me:
One, two, three...

What did you whisper Gita?
What did you whisper Petroc?

Check that most of the class are on target through 'Safety of the herd' and ask one or two to share. Now use listening partners to share a single opening sentence and ask listeners to report back on good choices. Or, using your 'Fairytale-Opening-stretched-into-a-sentence', carry on and retell the whole opening scene (confident that everyone has got their own bespoke opening).

Apologies if working through that very young pupils scenario was a little long-winded, it is the principles beneath the exercise that I'm trying to convey.

Let's look at exactly the same approach at work in a KS2 context.

Chooser boards to use in storytelling

Let's say we have reached the retelling of the Build-up of *Little Red Riding Hood*. Our storyboard is proudly displayed and so is our Good Storytellers success criteria chart (see page 10). We have recently been working on 'Language of Time' but have seen precious few time connectives actually appearing in the class written work. It is time for another chooser board!

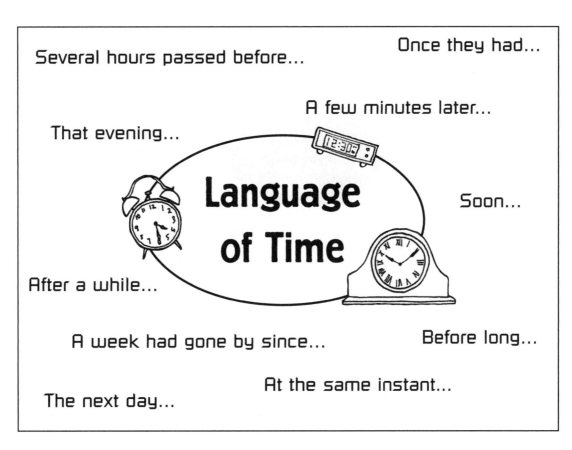

● Language of Time chooser board

(Yes, that little clock is important – we will come to that directly (See page 131.))

- Make sure that the class can read and understand the options.

- Ask everyone to choose one 'Language of Time' phrase that would be good to start the retelling of the Build-up. (Point to relevant picture of storyboard.)

- Ask everyone to whisper their choice to you. Check a few.

- Ask everyone to stretch their time-connective phrases into sentences.

- Whisper. Check a few.

- Now use listening partners to retell the scene, but this time the listener is not just looking out for 'What did my storyteller do well' but also 'Did they use a good "Language of Time" phrase?'

Can you see where this is leading? Almost any word or sentence level objective can be tackled in this way.

We decided that good storytellers 'choose good words' and we are now getting specific about exactly which type of good words we want.

We decided that good listeners 'think' and we are now asking the children to think about specific word or sentence choices from the storyteller. Below are a few more samples.

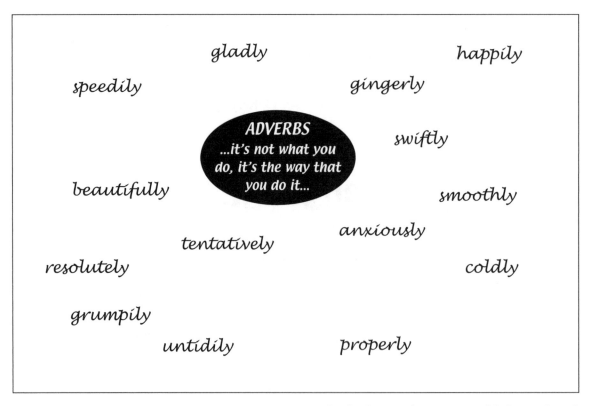

● Adverbs that can be very powerful chooser board

Of course, these boards can be *added* to – the word collection grows and grows. You can send the class on dedicated searches to find further examples for each board (a homework task that has some genuine usefulness!).

When introducing new chooser boards to the class, one way of encouraging a proper understanding of the new vocabulary is to play games with it.

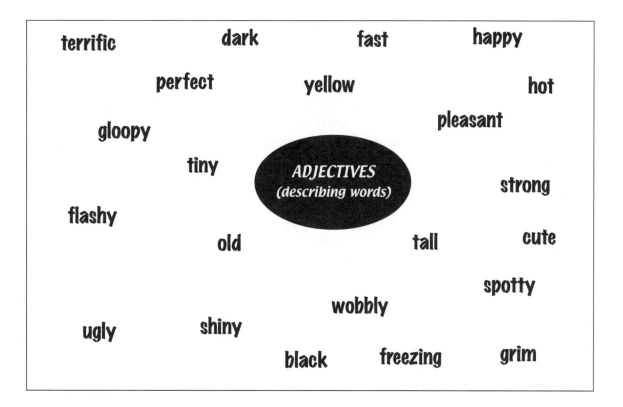

Chooser board 'Give-us-a-clue'

It is fairly common to see displays of useful words on the walls of KS2 classrooms (sometimes they are even large enough to be legible!). How can we make sure that these displays are not just irrelevant wallpaper but have real *meaning* for pupils and are actually utilized in their written work? Below is a very useful chooser board of words.

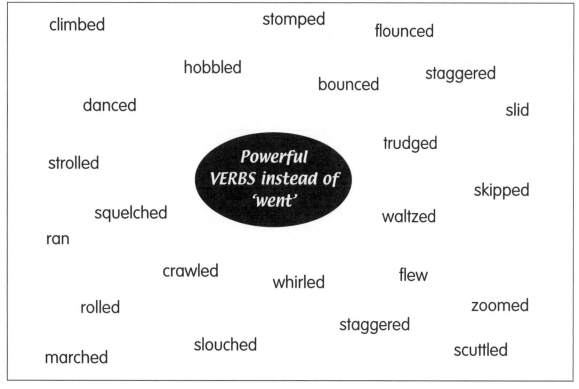

● Powerful verbs instead of 'went' chooser board

But do most of your pupils have any understanding of what most of those words actually mean?

Hmmm, probably the best way to begin is to start acting one or two out! Begin tottering around the room with your ankles close together, encouraging pupils to put up their hands and guess which word you have chosen (hobbled!). After a period of demonstration lurching, galumphing and sneaking about, it is the pupils' turn: 'Everybody choose one word from the chooser board. After three, whisper me your word… one, two, three… Now take a journey from your seat, around the room and back again in the style of your word! Go!'

Complete mayhem ensues for a few moments: 'Do the same again, but this time, on your journey, meet someone else and have a go at guessing each other's words.'

Now that everyone has had a go (in the 'Safety of the herd'), you can pull out particular individuals to demonstrate their word for the class to guess.

You can extend this sort of game to deliberately provoke debate by asking pairs of pupils to choose two words which are similar (such as 'trudged' and 'stomped', or 'danced' and 'whirled') and then challenge others to guess their words or spot the difference. Wonderful arguments about the nuance of meaning ensue.

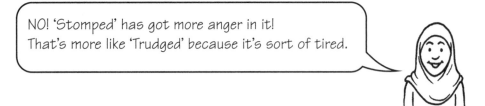

NO! 'Stomped' has got more anger in it! That's more like 'Trudged' because it's sort of tired.

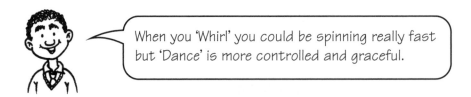

When you 'Whirl' you could be spinning really fast but 'Dance' is more controlled and graceful.

What is more, pupils get excited about their favourite words; they take ownership of the vocabulary and delight in using it wherever possible!

Perhaps 'Powerful verbs instead of "went"' is a bit of an obvious choice? You can certainly play the same sort of guessing games when introducing many other chooser boards:

- 'Powerful verbs instead of "said"' – get pupils 'bellowing' or 'whispering' or 'screeching'!

- 'Emotions/feelings' – how do you act the difference between 'gutted' and 'distraught'?

- 'Adverbs' – the classic game of miming tasks 'joyfully' or 'cautiously' or 'glumly'.

Chooser books

Some enterprising KS3 teaching assistants I was working with were very frustrated by having to change classrooms all the time. They could not put displays on the wall as they were forever on the hoof, teaching in different rooms. So, they invented the simple but powerful tool of CHOOSER BOOKS.

When I was at school, we had little word books that were supposed to help us to spell. We collected in words on pages arranged in alphabetical order. When the National Literacy Strategy first came in, my class had little word books that were also supposed to help us spell. We collected words on pages grouped by spelling patterns such as –air or –are or –ear. Both of these ways of collecting words might have some learning value during the process of collection, but neither is much real use once the collecting is done. They are hardly ever referred back to or used during speaking or writing tasks.

In a chooser book the words are grouped according to the job they do. If you want a good 'feeling' word or a 'powerful verb instead of "went"', you can quickly dip in and find one. Pupils can add to or personalize their books. Teachers can set spoken or written tasks and suggest: 'Have your chooser books open at "words instead of 'and'" while you do this task.'

Remember to ensure that listeners (or response partners) give feedback on successful or effective use of words from the book.

When we finally get around to writing, these chooser boards or books are going to prove invaluable for embedding our word and sentence work within the structure of our writing (see page 118).

But once again, before we stampede into getting them writing, there's still a lot more purposeful, constructive *fun* to be had first.

Chapter **4**

Creativity

▶ ## The ideas factory

Imagination versus reality

Some people seem to be pretty sure that they have a firm grip on reality. Where do they get their confidence from? Presumably, they find out about reality from a combination of the TV, other media and social interaction. We constantly receive messages from the world that help us build our 'world picture'. We are also constantly telling and listening to little tales and anecdotes that confirm or subtly alter the way we see the world. 'That's just the way it is' we say with complete confidence. Well, you'd have to be confident, because if you started to doubt reality you would be a loony, wouldn't you?

Or perhaps, you'd be a *child*!

Children, by definition, are growing, learning, finding out and making their own decisions about what is real and what is not. The last thing we want to do is present them with a tried-and-tested bundle of facts, figures and laws saying, 'That's just the way it is.'

Surely, it is our duty as educators to keep open that child-like sense of wonder and questioning? Open-ended explorative behaviour, fantasizing about possibilities and playing through imaginary scenarios are perhaps the real abilities that actually distinguish humans from other animals. We want the classroom to be a place where anything is possible – where mermaids can swim, where wolves can talk and where we can all invoke magical powers if necessary.

Do you think we are talking about an infant classroom? No, we are not. Perhaps all teachers should be dedicated to holding back the tide of reality that threatens to suffocate our youngsters from such an early age. If they are going to have to cope with the real world someday, all the more reason to give them as wide ranging a set of experiences and strategies as possible while they are relatively 'safe'.

Intelligence is, perhaps, the ability to come up with creative solutions in new contexts. The more rapidly the world changes the more our kids will need their imagination and resourcefulness to cope with it.

'But my class are just so unimaginative!' I hear you cry. Trying to squeeze ideas out of a class can sometimes seem a bit like getting blood from a stone. Yet what is our job as teachers? If our pupils cannot do something, it is our job to teach them how to do it!

Can imagination be taught? Maybe creativity is like a muscle – it needs the right kind of regular exercise to grow strong. Perhaps there are ways we can cultivate our pupils' spontaneity? A great book to read on the subject of creativity and spontaneity is Keith Johnstone's *Impro for Storytellers* (1981). Many of the ideas that follow are developed from his work.

Just imagine if all human beings were actually ideas factories – relentlessly churning out a million new ideas every second. What if our minds do actually work that way – sparkling new ideas forever bubbling up to the surface?

If that is true, where do all these ideas go? What happens to all this effortless creativity? Perhaps they never quite reach the light of day because we have spent our whole lives developing very effective censorship methods that prevent them from emerging. Perhaps your pupils are terrified that their idea won't be good enough, funny enough, clever enough, original enough.

You know that many of the pupils in your class have never had anyone say 'That's a good idea!' to them in all their life. Instead, people have always said 'Don't be daft!', 'You talk such rubbish!', 'That's a stupid idea!' or just 'Sit down and shut up!'.

Well, before long, you do not need the external voices any more because you can 'hear' the negative comments in your own mind before you even open your mouth. In fact, you have trained up your own little team of internal thought-policemen who run around inexorably squashing any initiatives (thus saving you from 'making a fool of yourself').

As adults most of us are very reluctant to expose our ideas in public; we are severely worried that everyone else will discover just how boring or dim or weird or psychotic we are. Yet we expect kids to do it all the time! Our job as teachers is to make it safe for pupils to have ideas and to nurture the developing imaginations in our care.

So here's some fun stuff to do which will help de-clog your own imagination while also encouraging a culture of creative collaboration in your classroom (wow, alliteration!).

Imaginary objects

Working with imaginary objects is great! They do not involve going into role or acting – they are just about the smallest piece of 'Let's pretend' you can have. For example, rather than 'Imagine you are an elephant!', try 'Imagine I'm holding a jelly baby!' – a much easier challenge to begin with!

Imaginary objects are easily accessible, very cheap and don't make any mess – what could be better? They are a great way to develop an 'anything could happen' atmosphere of excitement.

The best way to start is probably the good old MAGIC BAG.

- Tell the class that in front of each of them is an invisible magic bag.
- Ask them to take hold of their own bag, open the top, plunge a hand inside and have a feel about.
- Ask everyone to take hold of an imaginary object, pull it out of the sack, hold it up and show it to you.
- Tell the class that after a count of three they are to whisper to you what they are holding ('Safety of the herd').
- One … two … three…
- Now instead of 'come up with a good idea', you can ask individuals to whisper.

The 'creating' has been done previously in the 'Safety of the herd', now all they have to do is share that idea. If the group still feels a little inhibited, you can coax them by asking them to pull something lovely out of the bag or something small and precious.

As they grow in confidence, you can begin to expand the remit of the bag.

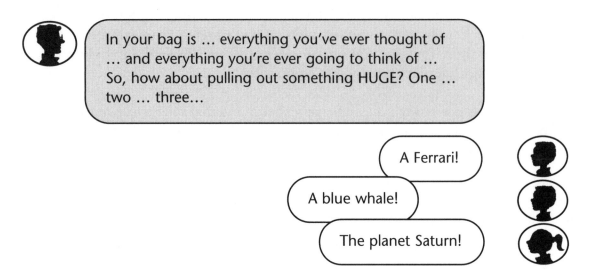

The scenario opposite shows how that process can be greatly enhanced by you, as teacher, accepting and affirming pupils' ideas.

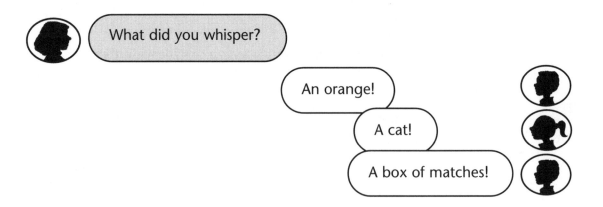

May I see your orange? (*carefully take and sniff 'orange'*) Hmm, smells nice … Can I peel it?

No!

Say 'Yes'!

Yes!

Thanks! (*peel imaginary orange and share the segments*)

Yum, yum!

Make sure all the pips go in this bin! (*hold out imaginary bin for pupil to spit pips into*)

Let me see that cat. (*carefully take 'cat'*) Isn't she lovely? (*stroke cat*) What's she called?

Dunno!

Hang on, it's written on her collar … Look closely … What letter does it begin with? (*point at imaginary collar*)

B…

Next?

L …O … O … P … Y!

BLOOPY! What a fabulous name for such a gorgeous cat!

May I see your box of matches?

Yeah!

Shall we set light to something? (*take 'matches', open box and begin striking them with pyromaniac glee*)

Yeah!

Let's set light to … ourselves! … the school! … the whole world!

Yeah!

(*Hand out matches, everyone mimes setting light to themselves and being consumed by fire while cackling demonically!*)

Now, the third example in the scenario is pretty close to the bone – it's just what happened to come out while I sat here writing away. I was tempted to censor it: 'You can't go encouraging pyromania in schools! Someone might be reading this whose school was burned down by arsonists or, worse, who've lost family and friends in fires!' Everyone can set their own comfort zone here – we probably do need to censor contributions on the (very rare) occasions that things get too scatological or sexual. Something like 'I think we all know what is appropriate and what is *not* appropriate in school' should be enough.

But, the truth is that accepting and going with the 'matches' scenario above is probably good practice and could even be 'therapeutic' for pupils. If children know that even high-status adults (such as teachers) have daft ideas flitting through their heads, then it makes them less ashamed of their own murky thoughts. Perhaps acting out dark fantasies in such a spontaneous way might make potential pyromaniacs far less likely to actually go through with it!

By the way, what do you do about the determined cynic who tries to stop the fun by saying: 'But there's nothing there!' You smile delightedly and agree: 'That's right it's an *imaginary* object; we're *pretending!*' Then carry on concentrating on those in the group who are game. Never waste energy on cynics; they can suck you down into their black hole if you are not alert. The best tactic is to outnumber them – play to your friends on either side of them. Soon, even hardliners will realize that everyone else is having fun and start joining in – then you can give them plenty of rewarding attention.

The Magic Bag 15-second Challenge

To really get people's brains frying, set a challenge.

> Who can pull the most objects out of the bag in 15 seconds?
>
> Rule: each object must be held up, shown to me and named out loud.
>
> Ready? ... Steady? ... Oh, and you know that object you were planning to start with? You're not allowed that one! ... Go!

Chaos ensues.

After 15 seconds, ask the group what that experience is like.

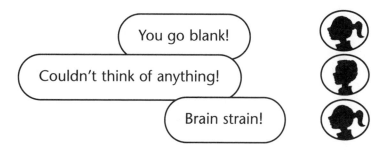

You go blank!

Couldn't think of anything!

Brain strain!

Perhaps the task was too narrow? Perhaps we need a wider set of possible correct solutions? Is 'everything you've ever thought of' not a big enough option? No, of course, the opposite is true. Our mind goes into 'brain-boggle-shut-down', overloaded by the amount of possibilities. With a smaller set of answers the task becomes very easy.

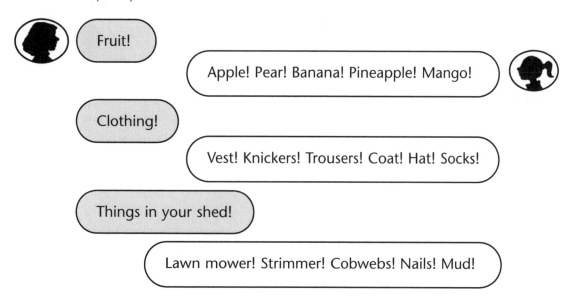

Fruit!

Apple! Pear! Banana! Pineapple! Mango!

Clothing!

Vest! Knickers! Trousers! Coat! Hat! Socks!

Things in your shed!

Lawn mower! Strimmer! Cobwebs! Nails! Mud!

This may seem obvious but is actually an EPOGI (educational principle of great importance):

In order to help people succeed with creative tasks it often helps to narrow down the choices available to them.

Then, as they become more proficient we can widen the possibilities. For example, which task is easier:

1 Write a story – it can be about anything you like.

2 Write a story following the basic plot of *Little Red Riding Hood* but set it either

   a) at the North Pole, or

   b) on a distant asteroid.

Another way to make the Magic Bag 15-second Challenge more achievable is by emphasizing its kinesthetic component. Instead of trying to think up another new idea, just put your hand(s) out and grab one!

There are as many different ways of picking up objects as there are ways to position your hands. So, get the class to explore as many different ways of picking something up as possible and then name the object once you've grabbed it.

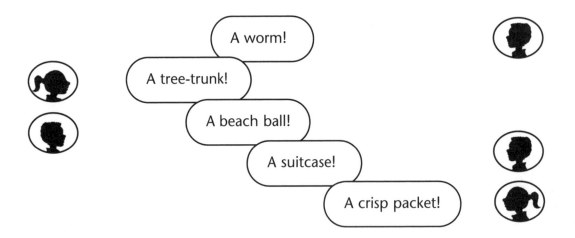

These do not have to be Marcel Marceau mimes! Just play with the variety of holding out and let the physical shape jog your brain. Whenever you want a whole variety of suggestions/answers from a class, you will get far better results by using the Magic Bag.

Instead of: 'What did you get for Christmas? Hands up!'
Try:

Magic bags everyone!
Pull out ... your favourite Christmas present.
Play with it a little...
Show it to your neighbour.
Now, who wants to show their present to me?

Instead of: 'Who can name a three-dimensional solid? Hands up!'
Try:

Magic bags!
Everyone pull out ... a three-dimensional solid.
Have a good look at it...
What shape are its faces? Can you count them?
Describe the solid to your neighbour and see if they can guess the name of it.

Instead of: 'What materials shall we test? Hands up!'
Try:

Magic bags!
Pull out three different materials that you'd like to test.
Find out what three things your neighbour has got.
Now tell me.

Of course, magic bags are somewhat restricted to objects. But this can be useful too. If you tell me what your object is by using one word only, then that word is guaranteed to be a noun.

In fact, magic bags are great for learning parts of speech.

 Can you pull it out of your magic bag?

'Dinosaur!' Yes! It's a noun!

'Cloud!' Yes! It's a noun!

You can develop this parts of speech idea by adding a second word that describes your object.

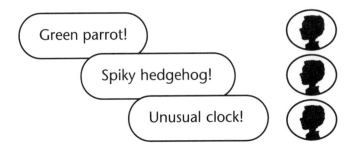

Or, get the class to animate their objects and add a 'doing' word (that's classroom-speak for a 'verb').

Remember to keep using 'Safety of the herd' through all of this, so that everyone can mumble, rehearse and make mistakes before sharing. (If you generate words in this way and then write them out on slips of paper, cut up the slips and play around with rearrangements, you generate some seriously odd poetry!)

▶ Collaborative creativity

Swaps

A very simple activity that builds into a genuinely useful set of tasks is swapping imaginary objects. Just ask the group to hold out an object and whisper the single word. Now model the swapping process. The top of the next page is an example if your object is a toaster.

- Go up to a pupil and say: 'Toaster?'

- The pupil replies 'Thank you' and takes the 'toaster'.

- They then hold up their object and say the name of their object, such as: 'Goldfish?'

- You reply: 'Thank you' and take their 'goldfish'.

- Now you wander off to another pupil and offer them the 'goldfish'.

- The first pupil wanders off and swaps the 'toaster'.

- Everyone joins in wandering about and swapping their objects.

You will be amazed how long a class will be happy to play this game for! After a whole lot of swapping, bring the class back to a focus and ask individual pupils to present their object.

Show and tell

This exercise provides a safe and supportive way to begin 'speaking to a large audience'. Many of us are intimidated by having to give speeches. The exercise paves the way to share news, report to the class, 'show and tell' and storytelling.

Selected pupils are asked to:

1 *Take* the space – that is, step forward and choose the best, focused position

2 *Show* us their imaginary object – that is, hold the object up and make eye contact with the audience

3 *Tell* us what it is – that is, in this case speaking the *single* word they have been given with their object.

Speaking a single word may not sound like a very challenging task but be firm about getting it right. Unless each of the three stages is clear, separated and defined (1 *Take* the space; 2 *Show* the object; and 3 *Tell* us what it is), get them to do it again. Depending on how secure they are:

- if they fail to make eye contact, get them to do it again;

- if their object changes shape, get them to do it again;

- if they are not 'proud enough' of their object, get them to do it again.

What's great about this is that we can concentrate on technique without having to be worried about content. After all, if everyone thinks that 'ball' is a lousy offering – well it was someone else's idea anyway! Repeat the swaps with two words (adjective plus noun) or three words (verb, adjective, noun).

When the class are confident you can begin to introduce the storytelling element. Pick up a random imaginary object, show it to the class and make up some 'back-story' about it.

> My 'shoe' is very special because … it's got a secret compartment in the heel… and I keep deadly poison in there…
> Or
> My spider is very special because … it can do triple back somersaults … (*demonstrate*)
> Or
> My log is very special because it came from the very last tree to be chopped down in the Oogambi Forest … We're hoping to be able to clone new trees from its wood and replant the forest using bioplasmosyntheticwotsitosis…

Ask the whole group to do a 'Safety of the herd' along the lines of: 'My … is very special because…'. They should go off, swapping objects and, more importantly, the little story snatches that goes with them. It's important to emphasize that this is not a memory test. If you can't remember the 'back-story' that came with your object, then just make up a new one! In fact, encourage children to adapt, elaborate and add to the story fragment they are given.

When you come back to a whole class focus, keep the discipline of:

1 *Take* the space.

2 *Show* the object.

3 *Tell* us what it is.

But now the 'telling' has grown into the beginnings of a proper explanation or report or story.

Learning how to show and tell with imaginary objects in this way is very sensible – you don't have to worry about getting your facts right but can get on with the business of communicating!

Gifts

If you play Magic Bag in pairs, then the 'Receiver' gets to accept and perhaps do something with each item. Sometimes, the 'Giver' becomes stuck, holding out an object but going into 'brain-boggle-shut-down'. If this happens, the Receiver can help out by naming the object instead.

It's this 'offering and accepting' we wish to develop. Giving and receiving imaginary objects is a great way to encourage pupils to work together, pay attention to each other and accept other people's ideas. As you play Magic Bag, model picking up an imaginary object and encourage the class to tell you what it is by asking 'What's this?'. Whatever they suggest, you agree and say 'Yes!'.

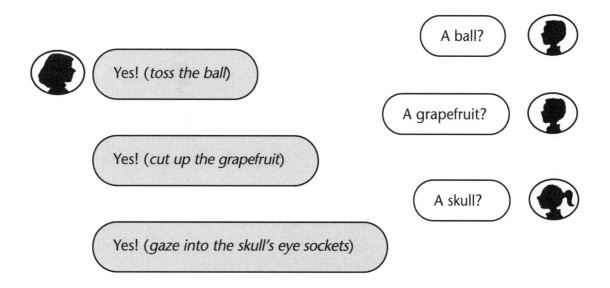

Now ask a pupil to make a 'blind offer' – which means to give you an object but without having decided what it is. Tell them that, whatever you say, they must reply 'yes!' Ask a few pupils to give you objects in this way (encourage them to offer very diverse shapes/weights/manner of holding) and then name the object from its physical attributes.

Happy Birthday

In pairs, Givers and Receivers can have a lot of fun making and accepting blind offers.

- As the Giver offers the object, they must say 'Happy birthday!'.

- The Receiver must then instantly name the object (no use of 'um' or 'ah' – just the first thing that comes to mind).

It's a tomato!

It's an aircraft carrier!

It's a grain of sleeping dust!

- The Giver confirms: 'Yes!'

- The Receiver must then show real enthusiasm and say joyfully: 'Just what I always wanted!'

- Press for real enthusiasm – otherwise cynics and competitive types will be tempted to sneer at or put down other people's offerings.

- The Receiver may now use, eat, play with, share, smear themselves with or climb inside their new object.

Tell the class to play this game in pairs, taking it in turns to give and receive – if necessary display a 'script' to support, similar to the one below:

Giver:	Happy birthday!
Receiver:	It's a…
Giver:	Yes!
Receiver:	Just what I always wanted!

Stand back and watch – when did you last see your class working so well together? They are engaged, they are motivated and they are collaborating!

Here it is!

For older groups, try this idea in threes.

- Person one picks up or arrives with an object and says: 'Here it is!'

- Person two takes the object and with great enthusiasm says: 'Ah ha! It's the … bottle opener … [or] donkey … [or] blancmange. Just what we need to…'

- Person three takes the object and begins physically using it in some manner, then completes the sentence: 'Just what we need to … prise open our brain pans! … [or] ride into Jerusalem! … [or] make into a snowman!'

- Persons one and two must agree enthusiastically and help person three to do the suggested activity together.

Performance skills

Simple games can be used to develop performance skills in the run-up to the dreaded Christmas play or similar. Instead of pupils having to remember (or more likely forget) the script, you can direct them to 'face the audience' or 'speak to someone at the back of the hall' or whatever is needed while playing the game.

Conclusion

So what are the main conclusions we've drawn about creativity?

1   It is far easier to be creative within clearly defined parameters – narrower choices, scaffolding and templates all help.

2   It is far easier to be creative in an accepting environment where people's ideas are welcomed, developed, 'free' and belong to everyone.

3   We can learn to extend this accepting culture to our own internal thought processes. We do not have to search for funny, clever or original ideas – the *first* idea is good enough.

▶ Collaborative storytelling

Let's imagine you have a good collaborative, creative culture going on in your classroom – what happens if you apply these ideas in a storytelling context?

Have you tried going around the class building a story one word at a time?

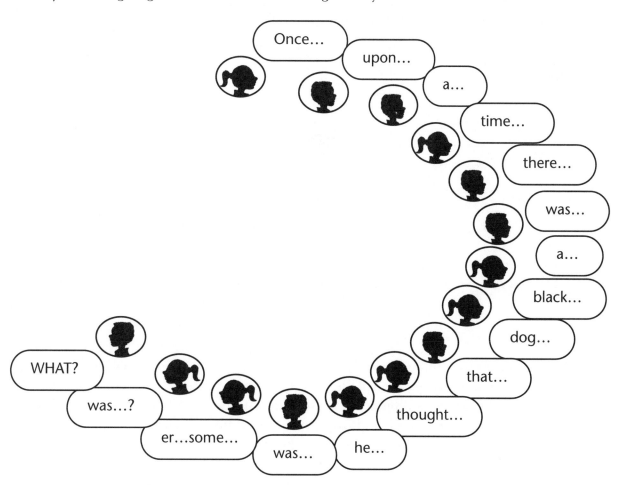

It's often quite difficult to keep the sense correct when pupils have only one word to contribute and they have to wait a long time for their turn; then, when it does get to them, they only get to say 'and' (especially when they were planning to impress everyone with their latest favourite adverb 'voraciously').

Have you tried creating a story a phrase at a time?

> Once upon a time there was another dog…

> his name was Jonah…

You gain more control over the sense of the story but it still feels pretty flat. The story fragment above is an example of 'full-stop passing'. Each contributor has finished their phrase or sentence and the next person has to build up again from ground level.

Instead, teach kids to do 'cliff-hanger passing'.

You can have much more fun with this. But there is still a major problem that occurs if you keep going for very long. Although the story is surreal, kooky and superficially entertaining, it has no shape or structure. New characters and events come thick and fast, and after the Apaches have driven off in the pushchair belonging to the Chinese octopus, you do start to wonder what happened to the poor old hairy rhinoceros who started it all off.

The story needs structure or it is not a story at all. But that's OK. You have got structure, remember – you have your trusty storyboards.

Play 'phrase at a time cliff-hanger passing' with a storyboard to follow. Make sure every item in one picture is mentioned before you pass on to the next picture. You will find that even though you detour and embellish, the pictures keep pulling you back to the main plot and produce a far more satisfactory story.

Here's a collaborative retelling from the Build-up of *Little Red Riding Hood.*

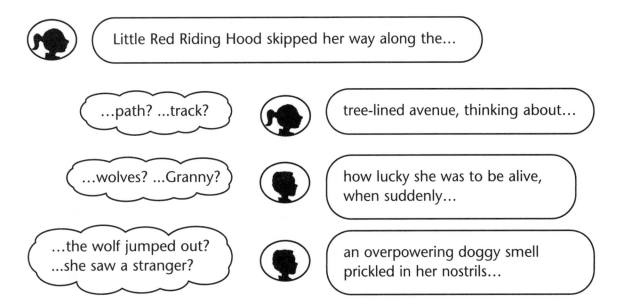

It's great fun to play this as Story Tag with two or three or more people, tagging each other to pass the story on at cliff-hanger moments. Or, (as Story Tag has been known to develop into Story Thump) you could try it with passing the magic microphone.

If a group of five or six pupils sit facing inwards (but with easy sight lines to the storyboard), they can tell the story among themselves. The magic microphone doesn't have to travel in a pre-ordained route – it can be handed back and forth about the group organically. If they are getting the hang of this, try replacing the magic microphone with a real one and recording each group's version of the story.

To turn this outward, back into a more shared performance, you could try Story Piano. For this, five or six 'volunteers' sit in a straight line facing the 'audience'. You stand behind them as 'piano player' – when you place a hand on their shoulder they must pick up the story thread. The instant you lift your hand they must stop. If the plot goes off track somewhat, the piano player can add a bit to bring it back on course. You can train up pupils to be piano players too. This performance produces great concentration and focus as everyone strives to follow every word.

▶ Tableaux

The word 'tableau' is used here to mean a physical representation 'sculpted' out of people. Very simple to do, highly motivating and great fun, tableaux build real empathy and understanding and have a myriad of uses.

- It's good to start from an emotional understanding. For example, ask the whole class: 'How do you think Little Red Riding Hood felt when she first set eyes upon the Wolf?'

- After a few seconds thinking time, invite the class to tell you what they thought.

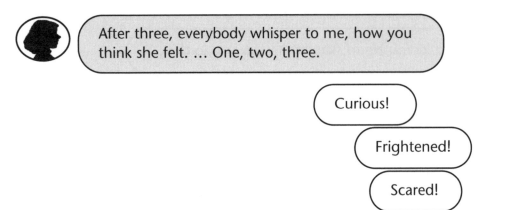

After three, everybody whisper to me, how you think she felt. … One, two, three.

Curious!

Frightened!

Scared!

Mumble mumble!

Interested!

- Collect in a few contributions.

What did you whisper?

'Scared!'

I like the way that when you said 'scared', you made a 'scared' face too. Everyone, after three, show me a 'scared' face. … One, two, three. (*clap, then pretend to take photos with imaginary digital camera*)

- Pick out some good features: 'Most people have open mouths. Look how wide Taj's mouth is! Lots of people have gone for eyebrows lifted. Have a look at Tracey's eyebrows – they're nearly over the top of her head!'

- Now with people feeling comfortable to be 'looked at', encourage a 'volunteer' (carefully picked) to come out to the front: 'I noticed that you used your hands not just your face, could you show us again?'

- Ask permission and keep talking to the volunteer as you manipulate them: 'Is it alright if I just take your arm and place it … here? Then I'm just putting my hands on either side of your head to gently tilt your head over … like that …' If you are gentle but firm, the volunteer will tend to stay in position like a life-sized action man or Barbie doll.

- Ask for suggestions from the floor: 'Shall we have the hand in front of the mouth … Like this? Or where do you think it should go?'

- Try asking a second volunteer to come out and practise being a 'sculptor', so reinforcing the 'gentle' way of working.

- Then, in pairs, allocate 'sculptor and statue': 'Right sculptors, you have two minutes only to build me a statue of Little Red (could be 'scared', or 'curious', or 'pleased' or whatever you prefer) at the moment she sees the Wolf. … One minute …10 seconds 'til freeze … three, two, one (*clap*).'

- Move all the sculptors to one end of the class to look back at their gallery of statues. Pick out and praise particular offerings: 'Look at that great facial expression. See how Morwenna has placed Isaac's fingers as if he was holding the basket…'

- Now the statues can get their own back by becoming sculptors and creating a statue of a different character in the same scene (for *Little Red Riding Hood* it would probably be the Wolf). Remember to emphasize body language and facial expression to communicate feelings.

- After looking at the new statue gallery, ask pairs to combine their two statues to create a paired scene. The two most important points to think about here are:

  - Sight lines – who is looking at whom? Who isn't?

  - Distance – are the characters close together or far apart? What is the appropriate personal space for this moment?

  - Perhaps share a couple of particularly successful paired scenes.

- Everyone has now had a go at being a statue in the 'Safety of the herd', so we can feel fairly safe about asking volunteers to repeat what they have done, this time in front of the whole class.

- Having created a two person tableau, add further characters and each time engage the whole class by asking them to offer ideas in physical form.

- When you've done all the characters, start on the setting and objects; for example, the trees, the basket, the path and so on.

 Hang on! Something's missing from our picture! What?

The trees!

- 'OK Dominic, you come out here with me. Everybody else, after three you are going to show us statues of trees. Dominic and I are looking for some good ideas to help us … one, two, three.'

- Add more pupils as inanimate objects or settings: 'After three … one … two … three (*clap*)… Freeze!'

- You've created a great tableau of one scene of the story. Take a digital photo, quick, before they go wobbly!

If you go through the whole process as described above, everyone has had participating experience and will know what you mean when you ask for a tableau next time.

You could divide the class into groups, perhaps appoint a Chief Listener to collect the rest of the group's ideas. Set them the challenge of creating a tableau as a group. Do they need you to appoint a sculptor or can they self-manage? The following points are worth bearing in mind:

- Initially, unsupervised group tableaux will probably need a bit of teacher 'tweaking'; for example, the audience want to see as many faces as possible, even of trees, basket or path (inanimate objects have feelings too!).

- The audience want height, depth and breadth with strong and weird shapes (even if we don't know what they're meant to be!).

- The audience want a disciplined 'freeze' (giggling is like letting the air out of a balloon – it goes all wobbly and useless).

It does not take long for groups to get pretty good at it. Remember to ask them how well they worked together. Celebrate the success of groups that collaborate well.

Each group could produce a 'before' and 'after' tableau or a tableau to predict how they think an unfinished story could end.

If you give each group one scene from the storyboard of the story you are currently working on, then you can present them in order to show the whole plot. Take digital photos and add speech bubbles and narration – what a simple and effective, collaborative multimedia presentation. Or perform it for an audience – there's Friday's assembly sorted!

Tableaux vivante

One way of extending tableaux is by allowing each person to have a movement cycle that continually repeats.

This works particularly well for inanimate objects such as waves continually breaking, flames flickering and trees blowing in the wind. It's a bit harder for characters because you want them to stay in the same moment and not move the plot on. But they can, for instance, repeatedly comb their hair, grumble under their breath, pace back and forth. It's fun to add sound effects that can be provided by the performer or be added by people off-stage. Challenge sound effect providers to match their sounds to the movements of the person on-stage.

Freeze-frame

The next development from this is to begin to act out the story. If you ask children to act out a story, they will tend to rush at it and barge through the entire plot in three seconds, scruffily interacting and losing many of the 'magic moments'. So, we need to slow them right down.

In freeze-framing, the characters are allowed to move the plot forwards in slow motion while you count one, two, three. Then they freeze when you clap. Then, once again, they move in slow motion while you count to three. This is repeated until the scene is completed, or you've had enough!

It is possible to present an entire story in this manner but it can get pretty wearisome!

A major reason for using freeze-frame is that it gives pupils a real experience, which is a crucial basis for successful hot seating.

▶ Role play

Hot seating

Hot seating simply means interviewing someone while they are in role as someone else. This can be a painful grind; here we are deliberately putting children in the spotlight, so it is small wonder if they clam-up. But, if you set it up correctly, hot seating is a wondrous way to create depth of understanding and release creativity.

Teacher in role

Remember: 'Never ask anyone to do something you wouldn't do yourself.' One of the most effective strategies available to teachers is modelling, so put yourself in the hot seat. It is a mistake to think that you need costumes, props or wondrous acting ability to do this. In fact, all of these can seriously get in the way. You want to be able to return to 'teacher' at any moment so set it up by saying something like: 'When I sit in the seat I will be pretending to be someone else. When I stand up I'll be back to me.' Sit in the seat briefly but don't say anything yet, just 'be'.

Another mistake people sometimes make at this point is to start telling the class who they are, what's going on and generally over explaining. This leaves the class with nothing to do and is rarely convincing. So, after a few moments 'being there', just stand up again, return to your 'teacher' person and ask questions about the person on the chair using the third person: 'Who do you think that person was? What sort of person were they? Could you tell how they were feeling?'

You have now established that you can go in and out of role very quickly and easily and that the person on the chair is not you. It's good to get the class curious and prime them to ask questions, so that they take the lead when you go back into role: 'Why do you think that person was sad? Shall we ask them? James, will you ask them why they are sad?'

Initially, when in role, give cryptic or partial answers and see where it leads. If the lesson starts to flag, just jump up off the chair, go back to being 'teacher' and nudge it forward some more.

It is much easier than you might think to lead whole sessions in which you sit in the hot seat without a clue in your head who you are supposed to be. Then, as the children ask questions you answer off the cuff and gradually build up a whole back-story and scenario complete with a problem for them to solve. If pupils have seen you in the hot seat, they understand that it is not about 'acting' but just about answering honestly in some sense.

Paired hot seating

Another 'Safety of the herd' approach is for pupils to hot seat in pairs or small groups. For example, having 'sculptured' a wolf, the sculptor can then interview him on every subject from dietary details to daily activities to advice for the eternally hungry!

Taking part in a tableau or, even better, a freeze-frame is perhaps the best support children can have before sitting in the hot seat. The freeze-frame experience gives them something concrete to base their initial replies upon while they are building their confidence. It is useful to get people into the habit of saying 'Yes' so you can tell them they must answer the first few questions that way.

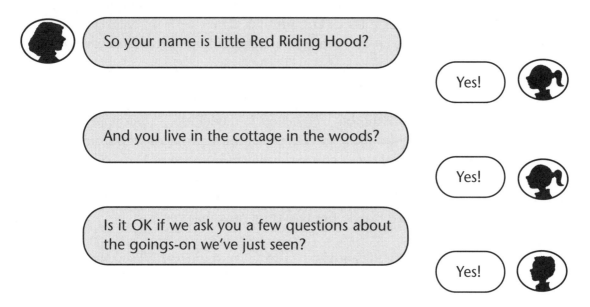

The next few questions relate directly to the bit of action that the child has taken part in so that they can answer 'truthfully'. Be deliberately hesitant, providing plenty of opportunities for the character to butt in.

 We first saw you, over there, you were … walking? What were you … up to?

I was walking along the path … towards my Granny's.

She seems to be settling into the role ... Let's get her to tell the story.

Could you talk us through what happened?

Well, there I was, walking along enjoying the flowers when suddenly I heard a rustling in the bushes ...

At this point you can just back off and let the child ramble, merely providing a nudge of encouragement whenever needed.

If you set a class the task of a 'First person recount' before and after this sort of exercise, the difference in quality of outcome is staggering. Most pupils need to see and meet a character (or, even pretend to be that person) in order to empathize with their point of view.

The next raft of questions can be very lateral and generate quality back-story: 'Have you ever seen a Wolf before?' Suddenly, the thought-policeman jumps in and the child replies: 'No!' This closes the options down, switches creativity off and stops things dead. So try the following:

Please answer 'Yes'. Now, have you ever seen a Wolf before?

Yes.

So, please tell us what happened on that occasion.

Well, I was out in the garden one day, the sun was shining and the birds were singing, when I heard a strange sound...

And off they go!

You can involve the whole class in asking questions but until they get the hang of what sort of questions to ask, it's best to filter the questions through yourself in the first instance. If they really get steamed up, there's no holding them back.

Some of the best responses often come from interviewing inanimate objects. You can discover the guilty secrets of a daisy, the tragic past of a bird's nest, the hopes and dreams of a pine cone. We were once interviewing a piece of string and wanted to find out about his life before he ended up in Tom's pocket. The child in role replied: 'Well, I used to work in the Post Office … 'course, I was a lot longer back then!' Great stuff!

Mini drama

Having previously worked in the theatre, it was immediately assumed that I would be a drama 'expert' when I first started teaching. Actually, the prospect of an hour-long session with everyone's shoes and socks off in the vast echoing hall filled me with dread!

The very idea of drama can be scary. So, try planning your drama session to start just five minutes before you know you will be saved by the bell. In fact, what is the smallest, shortest, safest drama session you can lead? The idea of 'mini drama' is that it is instantly into role and instantly back to normal – no one has to take their shoes off or move furniture!

Here's Robert, trying to write his story but feeling stuck.

Where have you got to?

Dunno what to write next sir… She's walking through the woods and she sees the wolf … then what happens?

OK, take this basket … (*hand over imaginary basket*). Look around at the trees and bushes … (*point out various imaginary trees and bushes*). Can you show me where the path goes?

Well, I think it goes over there … past that tree … and …

(*stand up tall and loom over child, putting on a growly Wolf voice*) Hello, little girl, what's a nice little girl like you doing all alone in these Dark Woods? What have you got in your basket?

(nervously showing contents) There's cakes and bread and a bottle of wine for my Granny 'cos she's been ill.

(*back in 'teacher voice'*) Well done, Robert. How did it feel when you first saw the Wolf? What thoughts were going through your mind? Now carry on with your story.

A classroom where the teacher is happy to plunge in and out of role at a moment's notice is quite simply a joyous place for a child to grow and develop.

Everyone in role

'Teacher in role' is a very powerful teaching technique. Once you are happy nipping in and out of role through mini drama and hot seating, you may be ready to plan a slightly longer drama in which you take the pupils with you into a fantasy situation.

One simple way of beginning such an 'everyone in role' drama is to get the pupils to hot seat you in role as a 'character with a problem'. If we stay with the *Little Red Riding Hood* scenario, you could choose to be Mum (whose little girl has not come home) or Little Red (who is lost in the woods) or the Wolf (who is concerned that nobody likes him). Remember not to overload the class with information and over-confess your problem – let the class tease the details out of you through questioning.

Once the problem has been clearly articulated, enlist the pupils' help in solving the problem. Back in 'teacher mode', lead a discussion about how the problem might be tackled. Divide the tasks up between small groups and find opportunities for children to take on the 'mantle of the expert'.

(*teacher mode*) Hmmm, so how are we going to help Mrs Hood to find her daughter?

We could go and look in the woods?

Aha … so you are saying we need a search party (*building vocabulary*). How can we organize a search party so that every bit of the Dark Woods gets searched?

You all stand in a long line and walk forwards together at the same time.

Right, thank you, Maisie, sounds as though you know a lot about search parties. When we are ready, do you think you could take charge of organizing us? … Hmmm, it is getting dark now. How will we see anything?

Need to take torches.
And whistles … so we can blow them if we find anything.

Yes, Greg, yes, Charlie. We will need all sorts of special equipment. Could you two draw up a list of all the things we are going to need?

In this way the question-and-answer session develops, deepening the thinking and strengthening the commitment to the fantasy. Small groups can be sent off to busily engage in specific tasks, such as drawing up maps, testing the radio equipment, stocking provisions, sharpening machetes, designing suitable clothing – the list is endless. Importantly, each task gives an opportunity for the pupils to take on a certain expertise and perhaps engage in some genuine research. 'Experts' can then explain things to the confused 'character with a problem' or to the teacher (who can gently challenge them or raise the expectations and so on).

Once you are ready to set forth into your fantasy situation, it is worth thinking about how you can make the best use of the space and the furniture. Rows of desks are great for 'Victorian Schoolroom', pairs of chairs build an instant 'Bus', a big empty space may be good for a 'Desert'. Perhaps a random scattering of desks will help you imagine bushes, trees and a wandering path among them?

The real power of such role play emerges when you steer developments towards some crisis or dilemma. As with freeze-frame, the skill is to slow things down, don't allow the class to zoom through developments but milk the moment for every drop it is worth. For example, the children are all in position, demonstrating in slow motion exactly how the searching procedure is carried out.

('teacher mode') After three, you are going to hear a rustling in the bushes, I want to see from the look on your face how you feel about that ... one, two, three ... And now, stepping out from behind a bush you see a tall dark shape ... (Wolf mode) 'Good evening, ladies and gentlemen, what a pleasant night for a stroll.'

Remember that at any instant you can pause the drama and click back into 'teacher mode' so that you can discuss how everyone is feeling, what might be the best course of action and so on. Try inventing a crisis or dilemma for the children to solve.

(Wolf mode) 'Little Red Riding Hood? Oh don't worry she is quite safe ... she is at my house having tea and scones. Why don't you all come too and join her? There's plenty of yummy things to go around. It's just through these bushes. Who's coming first? There's only room for one at a time...'

Here we are setting up some great opportunities for circle time activities and stranger danger discussions without ever having to deal with 'reality'.

Chapter **5**

Writing

▶ Principles for an effective writing culture

Here we are a very long way into a book about literacy and we are only now beginning to talk about writing.

This 'fun' stuff is all very well, but having told stories, drawn pictures and leaped about the room, it's now time to settle down to the more serious and important business of writing. Literacy isn't all about fun you know ... Now it's time to get down to some proper work.

Ha ha! Did you believe that? What a lot of rubbish! Why should writing not be every bit as much *fun* as any other activity? How have we managed to turn writing into such a grinding ordeal? How come so many 7, 11, 16 year olds and adults view writing as an onerous task only undertaken as a last resort when utterly forced to do so?

It is perfectly true that writing is difficult. It involves the orchestration of a whole set of skills: creating content, choosing vocabulary, constructing grammar, remembering spelling, forming correct letters, applying neat handwriting, using micro-muscular co-ordination and so on. Often, we forget just how many separate components pupils need to juggle in order to get writing right.

Just as it is in so many other learning contexts, the teacher's job is to deconstruct this major task into manageable, achievable, bite-sized chunks and then reassemble the whole. The challenge is to do so in a way that does not suck the life-blood out of what ought to be an enjoyable, expressive, celebratory experience.

Do you actually know how difficult writing is? Do you know what it is your pupils are tackling? When was the last time you sat down and wrote, for example, a story in 45 minutes? Very few adults in our society have done that recently and many would struggle to do it well. Yet, we still judge our schools entire achievements on this one outcome and also load our pupils with failure-messages if they are unable to master it!

Remember the maxim 'Never ask anyone to do anything you wouldn't do yourself.' Therefore, probably the most useful thing you can possibly do while your pupils are writing is to write alongside them. Whenever you have unaided writing time in your class, then sit the task too – both yourself and any teaching assistants. Share your process, your problems, your solutions, your pride in your own outcomes – these are massively helpful for pupils. Perhaps the main reason for having a teaching assistant in the class is so that they can demonstrate 'how to be a model pupil' – joining in, struggling bravely, sharing their efforts and demonstrating the learning process.

Ban the four-letter word!

Get on with your work!

She's done far more work than you.

When you've finished your work, you can draw your picture.

What message is implicit in these statements? It seems as though the school day is comprised of a sequence of work tasks. Each task must be laboriously completed before rewards can be earned.

Wouldn't you rather have a class that knew the answers to these questions:

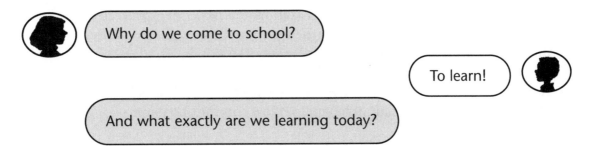

Let's not train our pupils into the 'world of work, life's a chore' mentality! Get rid of the 'W' word and make your class a place of *learning*!

Teaching writing

So how do we teach writing currently? Please indulge me while I take the mickey for a moment. The scenario of 'How to teach' that follows is based on what happened to me almost every day of my school career as a pupil. It is also pretty much the way we were taught to teach at teacher training college (late 1980s). Despite much good practice and enlightened developments, it is still the way many of us teach (although, obviously, not you personally, dear reader).

How to teach

1 Select your subject matter for the session.

2 Prepare an illuminating and engaging presentation that will grab the pupils' imagination.

3 Give your presentation with energy, verve and skill.

4 Hand out the books and pencils and say something along the lines of: 'Write about it and draw me a picture.'

5 Then chuck in a couple of reminders such as: 'Oh, and remember to use capital letters and full stops.'

6 Wander about the class nudging, helping, troubleshooting those who are stuck.

7 Struggle to keep rowdy class members on task.

8 After half an hour or so, collect work in and take home to mark.

9 Sit at home becoming more and more depressed scrawling red marks over book after book: 'Aargh, no capital letters, no full stops, what atrocious spelling! What's the matter with this lot? Was my presentation not entertaining enough, didn't I sweat enough blood?'

10 Next day, hand out the marked books. Move swiftly on to next subject matter and start again.

11 Repeat ad infinitum. Begin drinking to null the pain.

Of course, this is a mickey take, but how many of us recognize some elements of our teaching? Where in this cycle are pupils actually meant to improve their writing? That red-hot marking (which has gone icy cold by the next day) rarely helps a pupil make specific improvements, it just reiterates 'not good enough'! No matter how brilliant and stimulating our exposition is, by sending pupils off, alone with their bits of paper, we abdicate responsibility for the actual learning they need to do. We need to devise a process that is far more interactive and allows teacher intervention (and pupil reaction) at the point of learning. How can that be done?

We generally begin to teach pupils the belief that 'writing is difficult' very early on. Foundation and Early Years practitioners are some of the most resourceful, inspiring, important educationalists of all. However, it is also true that the first damage is often inflicted before pupils have even made it to Infants! Scarcely are they in the door, barely have they learned their teacher's name, hardly have they located the toilets, before we stick a pencil in their hand and get them writing.

Now this could be fine if it was all explorative, enjoyable play-writing. But we have all seen little ones, barely four years old, being 'corrected', being told to 'try harder', being given the clear message that they have got it *wrong*. This is not surprising if the following conversation takes place in most homes:

 What did you learn at school today?

I learned that writing is difficult.

Enough drip-feeding of this crucially important message that school seems determined to ram home and the conversation develops into something like this:

 What did you learn at school today?

Writing is difficult. I can't do it properly! I don't want to do any more writing. Why do they keep on trying to make me?

And here they are, all prepared and ready to come in to your class!

Some Year 6 pupils could accurately be described as 'militant non-literates'. They might as well be wearing T-shirts saying:

I can not write.　　**I do not write.**　　**I will not write.**

Our job then is simple. All we have to do is gently move our pupils from Box A to Box B.

But the trouble is, Box A is familiar, cosy and safe, whereas Box B is unknown, possibly lonely and certainly a long way away!

Happily, there are plenty of classrooms where a positive writing culture prevails. In these classrooms, pupils enjoy writing. They want to write and they positively clamour to be allowed to do so: 'Please, Mr Coleman, can we do some writing now?' Perhaps there is a magic wand to transform militant non-writers into purposeful authors? Perhaps not. Such changes are not about 'Elastoplasts over the wound', they are about deep changes in pupils' self-talk and self-image.

Long-term principles for a positive writing culture

Here are five long-term principles to help you create a positive writing culture in your classroom.

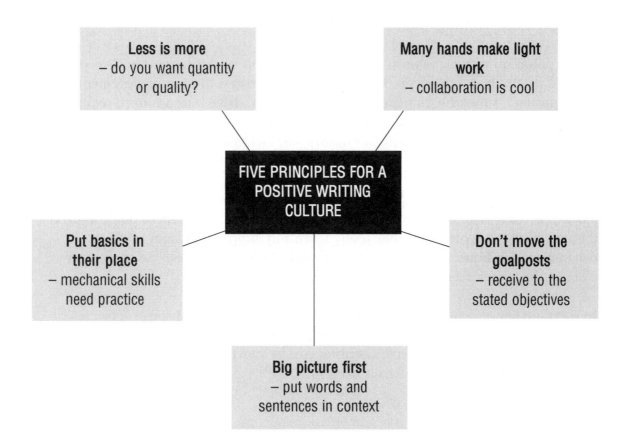

Less is more

Tom's teacher drew a small red mark in the margin of his page. She said: 'You can go out to play when you've written down to here!'

What was Tom learning about?

He was learning that quantity is far more important than quality. Rachel and Emily (and their mates) were already out in the playground having rattled out their daily two pages of neat, well-spelled (and perfectly mundane) writing. Tom (and his crew) has never finished a story or a report. In fact, he's never finished any of his pieces of work.

What if we said to this class: 'Please stop writing so *much*!' What if we set the goalposts very clearly on quality instead of quantity? 'You may *not* write more than half a page!'

For Tom and crew, this suddenly becomes a manageable task. Without the daunting prospect of acres of blank paper, Tom might just feel able to have a go. Rachel and mates must also adjust their approach. Instead of pages of rapid ramblings, they are challenged to slow down, to *think* about their vocabulary and content.

Wouldn't you rather have a single sentence of outcome that hits the mark and demonstrates successful learning than three A4 sides of fuzzy mediocrity?

Many hands make light work

Do you find it genuinely weird how our education system puts so much emphasis on unaided work? All final examinations are about solo effort and this trickles down to the heart of the learning process itself. Why?

Think about an achievement in your life – something you are proud of. Did you achieve that alone? I think probably not. All our greatest human achievements are collaborative. It took all 15 men to win that line-out, drive into position, set up two perfect rucks and feed the ball clearly for Jonny Wilkinson to slot that winning drop goal. Even Ellen MacArthur's extraordinary solo achievements are supported by a whole team of trainers, radio-operators and back-up crew.

Yes, one day pupils will find themselves in an examination situation, they will be judged on their solo, unaided efforts. But is the best way to get them there to drop them in at the deep end? Do they really learn anything useful from all those accumulated minutes and hours left alone with a piece of paper? 'Sit there and stare at the paper, feeling like a failure, for another 20 minutes!'

In the time between now and exam time, it is both sensible and constructive to support, scaffold and collaborate as much as is humanly possible. Gradually, the support, the scaffolding, the collaboration can be moved away and then the pupils will be prepared to go it alone as is necessary.

Don't move the goalposts

This is a very simple concept. If you have said that today's challenge is 'to learn how to use adjectives effectively', then *stick* to the use of adjectives when commenting on the pupils writing. We need to train ourselves (and our TAs and response partners) to bite our tongues and *not* point out the glaring spelling and punctuation errors that litter young people's writing.

Just because our writing was always commented on in this way when we were learning – does that necessarily make it the most productive way forward? Allow pupils to win the war, one battle at a time. (Actually, we will soon see how we can have more than one learning objective operating at the same time but the important thing is that pupils *know where the goalposts are*!)

- *Don't* comment on poor handwriting if receiving for effective adjectives.
- *Don't* comment on poor spelling if receiving for complex sentences.

Big picture first

Writing involves orchestrating skills on several layers at once. As good teachers, we do not wish to overload, so we deconstruct the task. So, today's lesson might be about 'how to construct a complex sentence' or 'verb agreement'. The problem with this is that without a context for the complex sentence or the verb agreement, it loses any point. It becomes a grammatical exercise and pupils are not engaged – they cannot see why such an abstract, arbitrary puzzle matters. You have probably heard a great deal of criticism of the NLS based on this point: 'Literacy has lost its fun.' 'It's all just "bitty" and reduced down.' The point is that it is possible to embed both word-level and sentence-level objectives within the text-level work.

So sticking with the example of story, children are engaged and motivated by the desire to retell. In our own retelling, we highlight how certain grammatical features or vocabulary have helped the final outcome. Then we set tasks for pupils to master these features (for example, complex sentences or verb agreement) within their own retelling. Simple idea, but does it happen in practice?

Put basics in their place

The mechanical aspects of writing – handwriting and spelling – are important. We have said that literary is about communication – illegible handwriting and atrocious spelling will seriously hamper communication – in fact, they might render a child illiterate.

Scruffy handwriting and poor spelling can be very annoying and offend our sense of propriety, but do they prevent communication? Try this very simple test:

Would you rather receive:

a) a well-spelled, perfectly neat piece of utterly banal content;

or

b) a scruffy and badly spelled piece of real passion and voice?

If you answered the latter then you probably are the kind of person we need nurturing the next generation of citizens. Many bright people, bright sparks, children and adults, have experienced torment and pain through their school career because they found spelling and handwriting tough. Even though these are individuals with plenty of original thoughts to communicate, our current school system tends to negate their contribution because the surface features of their writing do not match up to our norms. But the mechanical aspects of writing are important, and these people, especially, could do with plenty of practice to improve and develop their skills.

Perhaps handwriting and spelling need taking right out of the literacy lesson altogether. They need putting in their place. That place is daily practice, daily fun, daily enjoyable, physical interactive games that establish a basic mechanical competency. We often underestimate how much children themselves want to get better at these aspects of writing. It is not helpful to point out how often they get it wrong. It is helpful to give them plenty of opportunity to practise getting it right.

▶ Headlines and bullet points

Given the widespread use of bullet points, it is strange how rarely you ever see anyone teach 'what bullet points are and how to use them'.

Be honest, how many pupils in your class can't get the tense right, ramble on in sentences, end up writing the whole story in the planning frame? Or, once the main task is underway, never glance back at the 'plan' but go off in an entirely new direction altogether?

Yet bullet points and note taking are useful and powerful. For instance, when used effectively, they can help us both analyse plot and plan a new story. But the process does need deconstructing to make it accessible for most youngsters.

So, we shall now work through a (fairly lengthy) process that will lead to:

1 a plot analysis (of a known story) and then to
2 a bullet-point plan of a new story (a 'transformed' plot).

One way to help pupils (possibly no younger than KS2) to understand the nature and purpose of bullet points is to come at them entirely laterally by investigating headlines. Give groups a selection of headlines cut out from newspapers. You do need to deliberately skew the selection so that the chosen headlines exhibit the features you are interested in. You have, of course, given them headlines such as the following:

Huge bill for outside consultants fuels customer outrage

Crash pilot's father hails his brave son

Thousands march over job cuts

Celebrity chef cooks up a treat

Mike goes extra mile for loyal customers

Group fights proposals on forced retirement

Local MP stands down

This is not about word play and double meanings. (Do this exercise with adults and they get too clever but most children respond in an appropriate 'straight' way.) Ask groups to come up with three features that are the same about all the headlines provided. By collecting ideas, and perhaps a little nudging, you come up with criteria like this:

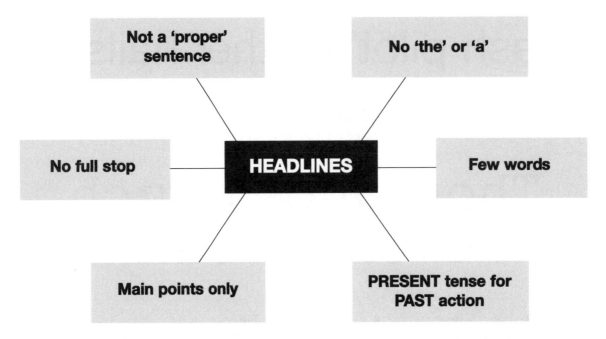

● Headlines criteria chart

We can explore these attributes a little further:

- **Main points of the story** – is the function of the headline, to summarize (and gain our interest).

- **Short** – is an important feature, we don't have to be a slave to counting words but they never ramble on.

- **Not proper sentences** – it is highly motivating to be asked to deliberately break the rules, to cross out the full stop!

- **No 'a' or 'the'** – headlines (and bullet points) rarely include any 'articles' – no 'the' or 'a'.

- **Present tense** – is the most elusive yet perhaps the most important feature. These events happened in the past, yet headlines refer to them as if they are still happening now.

You may have noticed that all the attributes of these headlines are precisely the same as the attributes of bullet points. So, to begin with, we set about working with headlines, but at the appropriate point (you are the best judge) we will seamlessly move into calling them bullet points.

Let's work through an interactive example.

On the whiteboard (interactive or olde-worlde), model writing a headline for the first scene of your story (as usual, do it 'badly', so that the class can teach you).

Little Red Riding Hood was asked by her Mum to take a basket of goodies through the Dark Woods to give to her Granny because she was ill.

Now, this is not a very good headline and the class will soon tell you why.

It's too long!

Cross out the full stop!

It's in the past tense!

So let's get editing. What changes do we need to make to get it into the present tense?

Little Red Riding Hood is [was] asked by her Mum to take a basket of goodies through the Dark Woods to give to her Granny because she is [was] ill.

Next, which words can we easily wipe out to shorten it, especially 'a's and 'the's?

Little Red Riding Hood is asked by [her] Mum to take [a] basket of goodies through [the] Dark Woods [to give] to [her] Granny because she is ill.

Don't forget to remove the full stop!

Little Red Riding Hood is asked by Mum to take basket of goodies through Dark Woods to Granny because she is ill.

Now that isn't a bad headline/bullet point and we could leave it at that. For older/more able pupils we might go further. Can we further shorten by changing the word order?

Little Red Riding Hood [is] asks[ed by] Mum to take basket [of] goody[ies] through Dark Woods to Granny [because she is] ill.

Which gives us:

> ### Mum asks Little Red Riding Hood to take goody-basket through Dark Woods to ill Granny.

You couldn't possibly expect children to come up with such a bullet point without helping them through the process step by step. If your pupils can jump straight to creating bullet points (present tense, short, not a 'proper sentence') then great! It just seems useful to go through the stages a couple of times before expecting them to do it in a single leap.

If you would like pupils to now create their own bullet points, first give them a rather long-winded, past-tense summary and ask them (in pairs) to edit it down into a headline. As an example, let's move on to the Resolution of Little Red Riding Hood (you know how it is good to get the ending sorted before fiddling with the middle). Give pairs something like:

> ### Just in the nick of time, the Woodcutter burst in and killed the Wolf. Granny jumped out from the Wolf's stomach and they all lived happily ever after.

Now tell them: 'You have three minutes to edit this summary into a headline.'

Here comes an important point – we keep the process 'interactive', so there is time to adjust, change, learn and succeed during the session. For example, as most pairs are finishing their Resolution headlines, we call 'time's up'. Perhaps, all the children read out their headlines together in a 'Safety of the herd' mumble. Pick out one or two examples to be listened to.

> ### Woodcutter kills Wolf, saves Little Red, Granny escapes, they all lived happily ever after.

Now give public feedback, possibly ask the pair themselves: 'How good do you think it is?' Or give a positive lead: 'Well, you certainly hit the main points.'
You could ask the class to help – pointing to the headlines criteria chart:

> Is there a way of making that headline even better by using one of the ideas on this chart?

> They said 'lived' and it should be 'live'.

> Thank you. Well that's easily adjusted – just get rid of the 'd'.

Perhaps the main reason for sharing in this way is to make good ideas available to all. So, after sharing explicitly, invite everyone to lift, borrow, copy the ideas of the sharer: 'OK everybody, if you wish to use some of the ideas shared, you may do so. Remember to check your headline for present tense. You have another two minutes "tweaking time" to edit your headline. Go!'

The headlines created can be transferred to paper. If you do have enough whiteboards, it's great to leave each headline on the board and end up with all four scenes each on a separate board.

Perhaps, your class have now got the hang of this and no longer need the long-hand summary first and then edit. Perhaps for the Climax you could allow pairs to go straight into creating a headline. You will greatly increase the chance of their success if you aurally summarize the scene for them first. Also remember to allow sharing and re-editing time so everyone can learn from each other. You might like to have each pair read out their headline to the other pairs on their table. Remember, you are training your class to give good feedback too.

Perhaps by the time you have got back to the Build-up, you think the class is ready for a solo, unaided challenge. Rather than 'alone with a piece of paper' for 20 minutes, this is 'alone with a whiteboard' for three minutes and pupils know that they will get immediate feedback from their partner or group and 'tweaking time' allowing them to adjust or change or cover their tracks before receiving teacher judgement. This is the most effective sort of writing task – short, sharp, to the point, very clear success criteria, immediate feedback and the opportunity to learn.

Through a process such as this, you have arrived at a scene-by-scene headline analysis of the plot of the story. Perhaps now might be a good time to cross out the initial capital, add a big fat dot and call them bullet points instead of headlines. So on your whiteboard, you can change your criteria chart as follows.

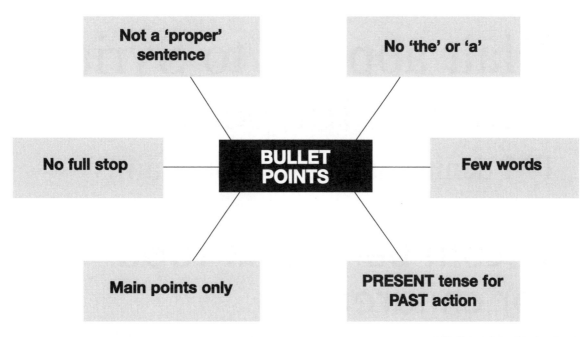

● Bullet point criteria chart

And your plot-analysis might look something like below.

Little Red Riding Hood

Introduction
- Mum gives Little Red goody-basket to take through Dark Woods to ill Granny

Build-up
- Little Red meets Wolf, tells him she is going to Granny's cottage

Climax
- Little Red reaches Granny's cottage, Wolf throws off his Granny disguise, attacks Little Red

Resolution
- Woodcutter kills Wolf, Granny emerges unharmed from the Wolf's belly

It is sometime quite difficult to get all the main points of each scene into a single headline/bullet point. But, once again, the solution is at hand, by going back to headlines. Some headlines carry subheadings underneath, such as below.

Sudan splits over role of UN in Darfur force
Mixed signals over peacekeeping in area where 250,000 have died

Blair appeals to Syria and Iran for peace
PM denies 'appeasement' claims

Ofcom bans junk food for children
No more TV ads for 'bad' products

You can use this sort of example to teach the idea that each frame of your storyboard could have several subheadings or bullet points, which could lead to the sort of example below.

Little Red Riding Hood

Introduction
- *Mum* gives *Little Red basket of goodies* for *Granny*
- *Mum* tells *Little Red* to *keep to path*
- *Little Red* sets off through *Dark Woods* towards *Granny's cottage*

Build-up
- *Little Red* leaves *path* to *gather flowers for Granny*
- *Little Red* meets *Wolf* who pretends to be friendly
- *Wolf* does not eat her straight away because he hears *Woodcutter* nearby
- *Little Red* tells *Wolf* that she is going to *Granny's cottage*

Climax
- *Little Red* reaches *Granny's cottage*
- '*Granny*' behaves strangely
- *Little Red* gets suspicious
- *Wolf* throws off *Granny* disguise and attacks *Little Red*

Resolution
- In nick of time, *Woodcutter* enters
- *Woodcutter* kills *Wolf* with *axe*
- *Granny* emerges unharmed from *Wolf's belly*
- *Little Red* decides to stick to *path* in future

We have, of course, already analysed our plot once by storyboarding it. There are some people (mostly teachers) who prefer to analyse in words rather than pictures, but the reverse is almost certainly true for most of your pupils. By analysing plot first in pictures and then in bullet points, you are leading them through a highly scaffolded process. As they become more able and proficient, then you can cut out stages and jump straight to the end product. But the real beauty of this analysis is just how easy it makes the business of story transformation.

Story transformation

As with most activities, it is probably best to model this story transformation process with a single whole-class example first. But, very soon, groups and pairs will be able to do it, and then individuals can have a go unaided.

Probably the best type of setting change to model in the first instance is one of complete fantasy. 'Outer space' or 'The Undersea Kingdom' are places where we can suspend normal rules and just get playful. So, what happens if we put *Little Red Riding Hood* in outer space?

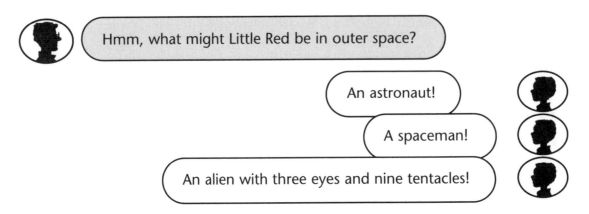

Hmm, what might Little Red be in outer space?

An astronaut!

A spaceman!

An alien with three eyes and nine tentacles!

Careful here – Little Red is our main character. We need to identify with main characters and care about what happens to them.

In fairytales, most main characters are young boys and girls – they are normal people called Jack or Alice. If you start off with your main character as something weird and wonderful, you get into problems later on. So, let's have Little Red as a spaceboy called Zip Electron.

Give each group an A3 sheet with the bullet-point plot of *Little Red Riding Hood*. Next give one member of each group a red pen or red pencil – you are going to use colour coding to make doubly sure that this process is foolproof: 'Now, everywhere you see "Little Red Riding Hood", cross it out and write "Zip Electron". As we've changed gender, we had better alter those "she's" to "he's" as well.'

Zip Electron

Introduction
- *Mum* gives **Zip** *basket of goodies* for *Granny*
- *Mum* tells **Zip** to *keep to path*
- **Zip** sets off through *Dark Woods* towards *Granny's cottage*

Build-up
- **Zip** leaves *path* to *gather flowers for Granny*
- **Zip** meets *Wolf* who pretends to be friendly

- *Wolf* does not eat **Zip** straight away because he hears *Woodcutter* nearby
- **Zip** tells *Wolf* that he is going to *Granny's cottage*

Climax
- **Zip** reaches *Granny's cottage*
- '*Granny*' behaves strangely
- **Zip** gets suspicious
- *Wolf* throws off *Granny* disguise and attacks **Zip**

Resolution
- In nick of time, *Woodcutter* enters
- *Woodcutter* kills *Wolf* with *axe*
- *Granny* emerges unharmed from *Wolf's belly*
- **Zip** decides to stick to *path* in future

Notice that we go down through the bullet points vertically changing all the occurrences of 'Little Red Riding Hood'. We do not go along the bullet point horizontally changing characters and setting as they occur.

Having gone through and changed the main character, pupils will be clamouring to change the supporting characters. You can push the thinking slightly towards the archetypal by asking questions such as: 'Who is the second most important character in the story? What role do they play in the plot? What are their qualities as a character?' Then ask: 'So what shall we have instead of a Wolf in outer space?' Give one member of each group a black pen or black pencil and ask them to cross out every 'Wolf' and replace with 'Alien'. You now get something like the following.

Zip Electron

Introduction
- *Mum* gives **Zip** *basket of goodies* for *Granny*
- *Mum* tells **Zip** to *keep to path*
- **Zip** sets off through *Dark Woods* towards *Granny's cottage*

Build-up
- **Zip** leaves *path* to *gather flowers for Granny*
- **Zip** meets **Alien** who pretends to be friendly
- **Alien** does not eat **Zip** straight away because he hears *Woodcutter* nearby
- **Zip** tells **Alien** that he is going to *Granny's cottage*

Climax

- **Zip** reaches *Granny's cottage*
- '*Granny*' behaves strangely
- **Zip** gets suspicious
- **Alien** throws off *Granny* disguise and attacks **Zip**

Resolution

- In nick of time, *Woodcutter* enters
- *Woodcutter* kills **Alien** with *axe*
- *Granny* emerges unharmed from **Alien**'s *belly*
- **Zip** decides to stick to *path* in future

Whole-class story-devising

There is a problem with coming up with whole-class collaborative stories in this way – many more people's ideas are turned down than accepted. It is easy to end up in rather frustrating head-to-head arguments over detail. So perhaps at this stage you might do more modelling – running your mental processes out loud, making your own choices and decisions and being clear that pupils will be allowed to use this technique to devise their own stories soon.

One fun way of doing this is to use the 'Find and Replace' tool to change 'Woodcutter' to 'Space Ranger', 'path' to 'space bearing' and so on. Remember that the colour-coding is not essential – it just sidesteps the possibilities for confusion that some pupils manage to contrive. Eventually you end up with something like the following.

Zip Electron

Introduction

- *Dad* gives **Zip** **neutrino fuel pack** for **his brother, Zack**
- *Dad* tells **Zip** to *keep to* **space bearing**
- **Zip** sets off through **asteroid belt** towards *Zack's pod*

Build-up

- **Zip** leaves **space bearing** to gather **gold nuggets** for **Zack**
- **Zip** meets **Alien** who pretends to be friendly
- **Alien** does not eat **Zip** straight away because he hears **Space Ranger** nearby
- **Zip** tells **Alien** that he is going to **Zack's pod**

Climax
- Zip reaches **Zack's pod**
- '**Zack**' behaves strangely
- Zip gets suspicious
- Alien throws off **Zack** disguise and attacks Zip

Resolution
- In nick of time, **Space Ranger** enters
- **Space Ranger** kills Alien with *photon laser gun*
- **Zack** emerges unharmed from Alien's slime
- Zip decides to stick to **space bearing** in future

You may not consider this plot to be high art, but if your pupils produced such a coherent plot unaided you would be delighted! They aren't about to produce a similarly coherent plot straight away, but you have given them a route map of how to do it. Perhaps after a couple of supported attempts, they will be able to do something similar unaided. Remember, it is for purpose and organization that the real marks are awarded!

Archetypal plot analysis

It is possible to go from this bullet-point scheme to an archetypal plot analysis. This is, conceptually, a little more demanding. 'Archetypal' simply means that you discuss the role each character plays in the plot and come up with a template story such as below.

Heroine

Introduction
- **Security Character** gives Heroine *valuable goods* for **Needy Character**
- **Security Character** tells Heroine to *keep to* **guidance**
- Heroine sets off through **dangerous terrain** towards **Needy Character's home**

Build-up
- Heroine leaves **guidance** to gather *attractive objects* for **Needy Character**
- Heroine meets **Baddy** who pretends to be friendly
- **Baddy** does not eat **Heroine** straight away because he hears **Hero** nearby
- Heroine tells **Baddy** that she is going to **Needy Character's home**

Climax

- Heroine reaches **Needy Character's home**
- **'Needy Character'** behaves strangely
- Heroine gets suspicious
- **Baddy** throws off **Needy Character** disguise and attacks Heroine

Resolution

- In nick of time, **Hero** enters
- **Hero** kills **Baddy** with *weapon*
- **Needy Character** emerges unharmed from **Baddy's insides**
- Heroine decides to stick to **guidance** in future

What should you do next, now that you have a bullet-point plan of a new story? Write the story? Well, you could and your unaided efforts would be vastly improved just because you have a coherent plot to follow. But, what you could do is convert the bullet points of the new story back into storyboard. This will then give pupils a concrete basis for aural and written retellings.

Transformed storyboards

Imagine that pupils have been working in groups of four. There are four scenes to a standard storyboard, so what could be more natural than to get one pupil to draw each scene?

Actually, there is a far more effective way to collaborate:

- Give each group a large (flipchart size) sheet of paper and get them to divide it into four.

- Give one pupil in each group a red pen and the responsibility for drawing the main character in all four scenes.

- Display your original (*Little Red Riding Hood*) storyboard and follow Little Red through the four scenes.

- Ask the pupil with the red pen to draw four Zip Electrons mirroring the facial expressions and so on in the original storyboard.

- Next, someone takes the black pen and does the same for the Wolf/Alien.

- Then a blue pen for Mum/Dad, a green pen for the Woodcutter/Space Ranger and so on.

All four pupils can be working at the same time, drawing this new storyboard and constantly checking back to the bullet points and the original storyboard to see if anything is missing. Any object in the template storyboard must have a corresponding object in the new storyboard.

● Example of transformed storyboard

With a storyboard of your new tale, you can retell it in various ways, use drama to uncover its secrets and so on. The more oral/aural work you do, the better the eventual written outcomes will be.

▶ Aural preparation for writing

Less is more

As part of your campaign for 'Less is more' try saying to pupils: 'Will you please stop writing so much?'

Just as you needed to boil an entire story down to just four pictures, so you can set a challenge about boiling a scene down into a strictly limited number of sentences. Tell your class that you are going to attempt to tell the Introduction from Zip Electron (or whichever story) in only four sentences (mentioning every item in the picture). Ask them to listen out for the full stops and count them. You might like to deliberately make your first attempt unsuccessful – we want them to think that there's a genuine challenge here!

Once upon a time there was a spaceboy called Zip Electron who lived at the far end of the solar system [*deep breath, full stop*]. One day his Dad called him into Mission Control and asked him to take some neutrino fuel to his stranded brother Zack [*deep breath, full stop*]. 'Make sure that you stick to the space bearing,' his father warned [*deep breath, full stop*]. So, Zip got onto his solar surfboard, strapped on the neutrino fuel and lifted off towards the asteroid belt [*deep breath full stop*].

Now, that's not a bad four-sentence retelling of the scene. You could challenge groups of four (having learned the difference between 'full stop' and 'cliff-hanger' passing – see page 86) to have a go at retelling, saying one sentence each before passing the magic microphone at the full stop. Or, ask listening partners to tell the scene in four sentences and count each other's full stops. Such versions certainly cover all the main plot points, but is the quality of the language up to much? Are we meeting our current word and sentence learning objectives?

Word and sentence objectives

You will want to make sure that word and sentence objectives are embedded in the big picture of a meaningful task (see page 103). Perhaps you've been studying 'powerful verbs instead of went' or adverbs. Make sure that the relevant chooser board is displayed;

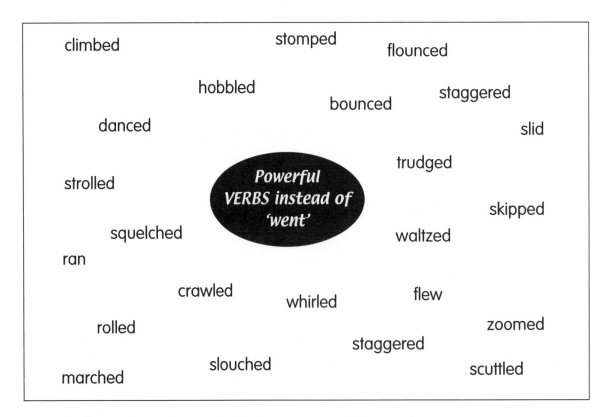

Use 'Safety of the herd'.

Everybody, look at the picture on the storyboard. Now, choose a powerful verb instead of 'went' from the chooser board ... a verb that you think you could use when telling the story of this picture... After three, whisper me your word ... one, two, three.

Check for understanding.

What did you whisper ... Eve ... Rupert ... Tasha?

Zoomed!'

Mooched!

Scurried!

Excellent. Now our job is to put that powerful verb into a sentence that fits our story. So my word 'rushed', I will put into the sentence 'Zip rushed into Mission Control to find out what his Father wanted'.
After three, whisper your sentences using a powerful verb instead of 'went' ... one, two, three. Now listen to your partner's sentence ... Hands up – who has heard a really good sentence we could make use of?

Collect a few examples featuring the desired language quality.

Zip *zoomed* off on his surfboard.

Zip *mooched* around with nothing to do.

As soon as his Father called, Zip *scurried* off to Mission Control.

It is worth spending time aurally preparing features of enriched language such as these. It pays real dividends in terms of quality of outcomes. We might rephrase the Storytelling Challenge.

> This time we are going to retell the scene in four sentences only and we are going to include powerful verbs instead of 'went'.
> Listeners, I will be asking you which powerful verbs instead of 'went' your partner made good use of.

We don't have to stop there – we could additionally go through the same process with adverbs. Then the challenge will become as follows.

> This time we are going to retell the scene in four sentences only and we are going to include powerful verbs instead of 'went', *and* we are going to include adverbs.
> Listeners, I will be asking you which powerful verbs instead of 'went' and which adverbs your partner made good use of.

We can keep layering these extra requirements until being allowed to write each sentence down is a blessing that frees up their brains!

▶ Interactive writing

Interactive writing simply means sessions in which pupils are working (perhaps collaboratively) on short, sharp, well-focused tasks, in which the teacher is forever interrupting, tweaking and engaging with the writing process at the point of creation.

Of course, not all sessions are interactive – at some point pupils will be performing unaided tasks. But this sort of interactive session is going to greatly increase their chances of success when they do strike out on their own. So, let's work through a process where groups of pupils collaborate in their writing to produce rich, concise fiction outcomes.

Do you often use mixed ability groupings or pairings? If the tasks are well structured, then such groupings can be very powerful. Less-able pupils get to contribute at their own level, more-able pupils learn reflectively through the teaching or supporting process and all pupils get to experience success.

We have done plenty of preparatory aural work on our newly devised story (for example, *Zip Electron*). It must surely be time to start on a written version. So, let's start at the very beginning. Are you happy with everyone using 'Once upon a time' to open all their aural stories? Maybe, at KS1 that will be appropriate, but surely we can do better? (See page 63 for using a chooser board to encourage variety in fairytale openings.) How about a chooser board of different types of story openings?

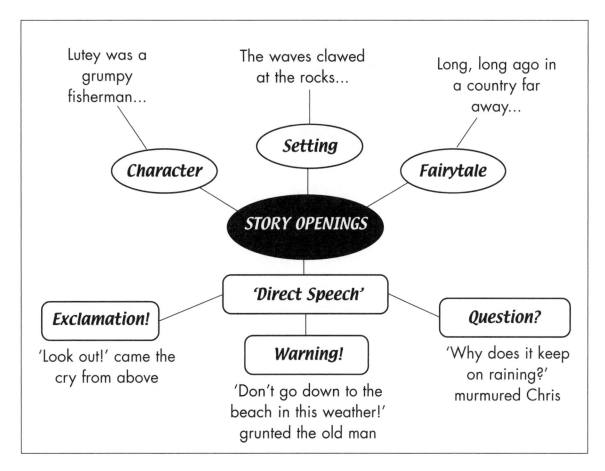

Let's imagine that we are going to further restrict the choices available (restricting choice aids creativity; see page 78). So, for today, let's say that all our stories are going to open with an effective description of the setting. Over the page is another chooser board of setting descriptions collected from the opening sentences of various stories for young people.

However, these phrases might not do the job for the particular setting we require. Demonstrate that, with a little adjustment, any of the phrases can be adapted for any situation. Write any given phrase on the whiteboard and edit, changing one word at a time to make a new phrase. For example, 'all was quiet and still' can become 'all was hustle and bustle'; 'litter-strewn streets' can become 'boulder-strewn pathway'; 'leaves dancing in the breeze' can become 'meteorites scudding through the emptiness'.

Ask groups or pairs to work together to choose a phrase from the board and write it on their own whiteboard (one pen, one whiteboard per group, initially). Then challenge them to edit it so that the new phrase evokes the setting of our new story:

silent expanse

ripples chuckling
against the bank

a storm brewing

litter-strewn streets

the houses tumbled
over each other

**Descriptive
language for
SETTINGS**

the sun beat
down

craggy precipice

a crimson sky

the waves
clawed at the
rocks

leaves dancing in
the breeze

all was quiet
and still

● Setting descriptions chooser board

I'm looking for the first group to be sitting, looking at me with a smug grin because they know that everyone in the group is pleased with their new phrase.

Check for understanding using 'Safety of the herd', or asking various groups to read out their new phrases. The challenge now is to stretch that phrase into a full sentence to open the story with: 'So I'm going to stretch my phrase "meteorites scudding through the emptiness" into a full sentence … "The stillness of outer space was occasionally interrupted by meteorites scudding through the emptiness." As a group, stretch your phrase into a full sentence. Pass the pen and whiteboard on to another member of the group and they can scribe the group's sentence. I'm looking for the first group to be sitting, looking at me with a smug grin because they know that everyone in the group is pleased with their new opening sentence.'

When you ask groups to share their offerings, it may become apparent that some have slightly missed the target. Use constructive feedback and sharing ideas to make sure that all groups have achieved this first small step: 'All groups, you have just 30 seconds "tweak time" to use the ideas you have just heard shared or to make other improvements to your sentence … Go!'

You have hit a bit of a milestone here – you have actually got something down in writing! In fact, every child in the class has got part-ownership in a cracking opening sentence rich with descriptive language. They may not have actually physically written it themselves but they have participated in the creative process that engendered it. It may just be in draft, on a scruffy whiteboard, but it has real quality!

Let's move onto a second sentence. Let's enrich our language by including some direct speech. You can refer to your storyboard, or, build a very simple tableau and ask pupils to add imaginary speech bubbles: 'What do you think Zip might be saying in this Introduction picture? After three, everyone whisper what he is saying, one, two, three … What did you whisper, Craig? …and you, Maria?'

Now give out extra whiteboards and pens (but still no more than one between two). For instance, in pairs, the 'scribe' holds the pen and the 'dictator' holds the whiteboard: '"Dictators" speak the words that Zip says in this scene. "Scribes" write down what you hear.' Collect and share a few examples. Allow a little 'tweak time' if necessary.

You have probably seen the whiteboard trick of teaching speech marks to younger pupils by drawing the speech bubble and then rubbing it all out just leaving the opening and closing marks.

Becomes

"I will do it Dad!"

Alert pupils to the fact that this sentence doesn't yet tell us who is doing the speaking. Suggest that we add 'said Zip' to our sentence.

Hmmm, perhaps it is time to reject 'said' and model writing in your choice of 'powerful verb instead of said' from a chooser board.

"I will do it Dad!" *announced* Zip Electron.

Ask pairs to swap roles of scribe and dictator and complete their sentences using powerful verbs instead of 'said' from the chooser board. Here we are at our next milestone – every pupil now has two sentences in writing (somewhere, on a whiteboard shared with others).

When sharing these sentences, it is good to request that pupils read both sentences one after the other so that the audience get a sense of the flow. Each pair can share their two sentences with the others on their table. Do the two sentences flow together? Have they hit the success criteria (for example, good description of setting, direct speech, word instead of 'said')? How good are your pupils at giving constructive feedback (see page 58)?

Perhaps you could transfer to paper at this stage? The main argument in favour of moving to a paper copy is that everyone has probably run out of whiteboard room. If possible, it is probably better to get a whole scene – a chunk (in this case, four sentences) – done before stopping to make a paper copy.

Let's carry on and get two more sentences done and then think about paper. For each of the next two sentences we can still give very tight criteria as to what it must include.

For the third sentence, to avoid the problem of all-talk-no-action, endless dreary conversations in children's writing, I have a simple rule. You are not allowed to use direct speech twice in a row. So the third sentence must be narration once again. Make the choice easier by making the choice smaller – narrow the criteria. For example: 'This third sentence must tell us how the main character is feeling and why.'

Luckily, we have a chooser board of good 'feeling words'.

cheerful

jealous

happy

curious

guilty   self-satisfied   fed up

full of beans   **EMOTIONS**   terrified

anxious   under the weather   gutted

amazed   concerned   glad

sick as a parrot   pleased

● Feelings/emotions chooser board

Ask pupils to choose a word and put it into a sentence. You might even add another instruction such as 'The sentence must contain the word "because".'

As soon as adults are asked to come up with a sentence, they pick up a pen to scribble. Many of your pupils are *not* at that stage yet. They probably need thinking time and aural/oral rehearsal first. So, once again you could ask pairs to collaborate – one picks an emotion word from the chooser board, the other writes it down. The second person puts the word into a sentence and dictates it back to the first person who writes it down.

 excited

Zip felt excited by the idea of taking his surfboard out into space.

You are cutting out all that 'Don't know what to write, Miss.' You are unpicking the stages of:

1   create an idea

2   test it verbally

3   then write it down.

We are also collaborating throughout the process. More-able pupils may find this frustrating – they want to be allowed to scribble away. But we are forcing them to slow down and consider and co-operate. This works as a reverse psychology – by the time you do let them write freely, they are wound up and raring to get at it!

Sentence four needs to be a 'mop-up' sentence – this is your last chance to make sure that you have mentioned every item in your picture and move things towards the next scene. So, let's recap our three sentences written down so far:

> The stillness of outer space was occasionally interrupted by meteorites scudding through the emptiness.
>
> "I will do it Dad!" announced Zip Electron.
>
> Zip felt excited by the idea of taking his surfboard out into space.

Now, looking back at the Introduction picture of our storyboard, what have we got left to mention? There's the neutrino fuel and the space bearing device and brother Zack. So, something like:

> So, he strapped the emergency neutrino fuel to his surfboard, activated the space bearing device and set off to rescue his brother Zack.

Having worked in pairs so far, you might declare that pupils are ready for solo 'alone with a whiteboard' time for this fourth sentence. You may consider that they no longer need to whisper in the 'Safety of the herd', or to rehearse with a listening partner – you might just ask them to write their sentences down.

Remember, by slowing the process down, you are setting bite-sized, well-structured, achievable tasks for the less able and you are creating a wound-up, desperate-to-get-on-and-write energy in the more able. Both of these are productive. Your professional skill and judgement as a teacher is knowing when to relax the structure and let them gallop.

Let's imagine that everyone has four sentences written on whiteboards – some collaborative, some solo. All four sentences can be read in sequence to a partner or wider audience. Listeners can give constructive feedback because the success criteria have been clearly defined. Pupils will be very keen to read their four sentences to the class, proud of their creations. Remember that ideas are free and in common ownership: 'Everyone; you have just 30 seconds "tweak time" to use the ideas you have just heard shared or to make other improvements to your four sentences ... Go!'

Presumably you would now like to get these whiteboard scribbles transferred to paper. Just before you do, could you ask yourself exactly why that is necessary? If pupils are keen to create a best copy – they wish to see their efforts 'published' – then all very well. But do you always have to create best copies of all the writing you do? Is not the process sometimes more important than the product?

However, if you are transferring to paper, you do have a chance to edit before you make best copies. Can you rush around checking all 30 offerings? No. Train your pupils to give good feedback to each other. There have been very clear success criteria for each sentence – partners can easily point out successes and suggest improvements (sticking rigidly to the given criteria). Also, this is the point where pupils may ask for advice or spellings and so on (from each other in the first instance) – if they want to.

Most pupils do want to spell correctly but go into shut down if overloaded with too many corrections. Ask them if they would like to change any spellings that they are not sure of (maximum of three for any one pupil) and bite your tongue about any others.

▶ Writing frames

Finally, after all this, we are ready to put pen to paper. But, what sort of paper? One day, we will be alone with a blank sheet. One day we will have to sit there and, mentally, go through a whole process similar to the above but condensed into a solo creative effort lasting, perhaps, one hour. But, in the meantime, we are going to use the paper to continue to give as much help, prompting and scaffolding as possible.

Opposite is a suggested writing frame for the exercise we have just been through.

Title: _____

By: _____

TOOLBOX	Introduction
You must: **1** Open with a description of the setting. **2** How was the main character feeling? **3** Move the action on using direct speech (alternative to 'said'). **4** 'Mop-up' sentence leading to Build-up.	

Date: _____

TOOLBOX	Build-up
You must: **1** Begin with 'passage of time' connective. **2** Move the action on using direct speech (alternative to 'said'). **3** What did the main character do? (strong verb) **4** 'Mop-up' sentence leading to Climax.	

Date: _____

TOOLBOX	Climax
You must:	
1 'Passage of time' connective.	
2 Move the action on using direct speech (alternative to 'said').	
3 Use three short sentences for impact.	
4 What did the main character do? (strong verb)	

Date: _____

TOOLBOX	Resolution
You must:	
1 'Passage of time' connective.	
2 Use direct speech (alternative to 'said').	
3 Link back to the very beginning.	
4 How did it all end up?	

Date: _____

I first saw writing frames used in this way by my good friend Dai Sweeney of Looe Primary School and owe a lot of these ideas to him. Notice just how tightly structured this is. The 'toolbox' actually instructs pupils sentence by sentence in a very narrow way. It's less of a toolbox than a 'prescription'. But, we go with the word 'toolbox' because, later, as we relax the prescriptiveness, the toolbox does become a set of suggestions rather than instructions.

This kind of writing frame will *not* work (or will not work *well*) if you simply photocopy it and put it in front of the class. It does need to be introduced, at first, through some sort of process resembling the above interactive session and including aural and/or whiteboard practice of each sentence. Later, you may choose to skip those stages. Remember, pupils are on a journey that leads to confident writing unaided on a blank page. They are just starting from a highly structured, very scaffolded, success-guaranteed place. As pupils grow in confidence, the scaffolding will gradually be removed until the pupils are operating independently.

If, at the end of a lesson, every child has four sentences written, four sentences that are purposeful, characterful, hit this week's targets, move the story forward, then I'm a happy teacher. You can always move on to the Build-up next session.

As children become more familiar with working on writing frames in this way, they can do so more and more independently. For younger pupils, it is important to keep giving visual reminders of what is required. Here is the first page of a Key Stage 1 writing frame.

Introduction	
TOOLBOX Fairytale opening Strong verb 'Mop-up' ☐○ ☐○ ☐○	

Build-up

TOOLBOX

Language of time

Strong verb

'Mop-up'

☐ ○   ☐ ○   ☐ ○

Climax

TOOLBOX

☐ ○   ☐ ○   ☐ ○

Resolution	
TOOLBOX	
□o □o □o	

Remember the butterfly icon (see page 63)? That means 'choose from the fairytale opening chooser board'. The little frog logo means 'choose from the 'verbs/doing words' board and the little clock means 'choose from the Language of Time board'. Try making up your own logos to help younger pupils know which chooser board to pick from.

What about the square, circle, square, circle, square, circle, at the bottom? Train your pupils to put in their capital letter and full stop to 'help them count their three sentences'.

What else might go in the toolbox? Well, you might want to relax the sentence-by-sentence prescription and just have an assortment of features leaving pupils to work out how to arrange them.

Marking

As we suggested, the problem with most marking (apart from the fact that it takes up so much of your precious time and energy) is that it has gone 'cold' by the next session and has little impact on pupils' learning.

With these writing frames pupils mark their own work (like a 'marking ladder'). You can even ask them to use a different colour for each feature.

Here is a Key Stage 1 example where the child is telling me that she does understand what is meant by a fairytale opening and she has self-corrected all her capitals and full stops without my saying a word – she was reminded by the square icons.

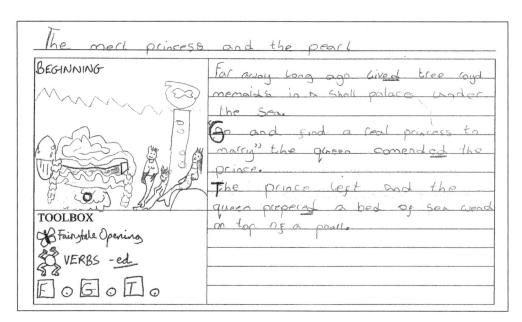

The meal princess and the pearl

BEGINNING

Far away long ago lived tree royd memaids in a shell palace under the sea.
"Go and find a real princess to marry" the queen comended the prince.
The prince left and the queen prepered a bed of sea weed on top of a pearl.

TOOLBOX
Fairytale Opening
VERBS -ed
F o G o T o

● Example Key Stage 1 outcome

Below is a Key Stage 2 example where the pupil has self-corrected when he realized he hadn't included any 'feeling'.

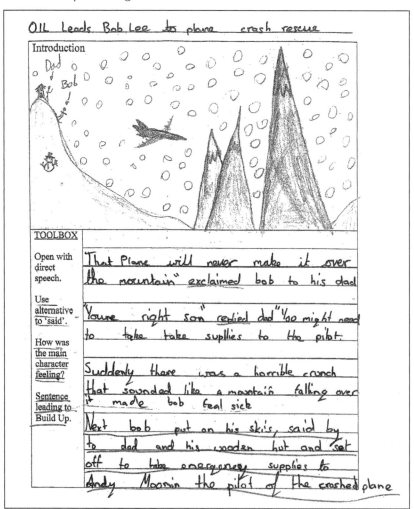

OIL Leads Bob Lee to plane crash rescue

Introduction

TOOLBOX

Open with direct speech.

Use alternative to 'said'.

How was the main character feeling?

Sentence leading to Build Up.

"That Plane will never make it over the mountain" exclaimed bob to his dad
"Youre right son replied dad "Yoo might need to take take supplies to the pilot.
Suddenly there was a horrible crunch that sounded like a mountain falling over it made bob feal sick
Next bob put on his ski's, said by to dad and his wooden hut and set off to take emergency supplies to Andy Moonin the pilot of the crashed plane

● Example Key Stage 2 outcome

Do you recognize the plot above? It's our old friend *Little Red Riding Hood*!

Brave Tales – Developing Literacy through Storytelling

Conclusion

Here we are, pretty much at the end of this book. How have you got on? Have some of these ideas been of practical use in the classroom? How is your teaching style?

Do you remember the mickey-take 'teaching sequence' on page 99? Let's come up with a revised possible teaching sequence and, in doing so, summarize the entire book.

Possible teaching sequence for developing literacy through storytelling

1 Choose your story and prepare to tell it (by scribbling your own storyboard).

2 Recap 'Good Listeners' with the class.

3 Tell the story (using own storyboard as crib sheet).

4 Respond physically (mini drama).

5 Establish 'What do good storytellers do'? Create a success criteria chart.

6 Produce a storyboard to map the plot.

7 Produce relevant chooser boards for word and sentence objectives.

8 Use listening partners to rehearse the story aurally, give feedback, improve performance.

9 Use whiteboards for first-draft interactive writing, sentence by sentence.

10 Use writing frames to structure written offerings – pupils evaluate their own (and peers') efforts and they inform you about their next needs.

After successfully retelling a known story, repeat the process with a transformed plot: imitate, innovate, invent!

Have fun!

An afterthought

storytelling for non-fiction and across the curriculum

The approach to literacy advocated in this book has grown from an initial storytelling perspective. As such, it might be seen to be concerned with just one small section of the fiction element of literacy (that is, traditional stories, myths and legends). However, it does not take a great leap of the imagination to apply the principles in a wider set of situations.

We have seen how fairytales offer a sound and manageable introduction to understanding plot. These plots can then be usefully transformed to deal with every genre of fiction. By removing the pressure to invent new plots, pupils can concentrate on the features of each genre instead.

● Example of Little Red transformed into spine chiller

But, it starts to get even more exciting when you go beyond fiction into non-fiction genres.

▶ non-fiction

> We don't teach fiction in our school – we stick to non-fiction because they tend to do much better at it!

Aaaagh! These are the actual words of a headteacher of my acquaintance! Those poor pupils are being deliberately starved of storytelling! Luckily, such a stance is uncommon (and against the law!) but do you see where this headteacher was coming from?

She believes that if she strips away all that fuzzy, amorphous, fictional stuff and sticks to what is concrete and real then the pupils (especially the boys) will be able to grasp the fundamental building blocks of the task.

Hasn't she got things precisely inside-out?

Hopefully, we have shown how fiction, too, can be very structured and scaffolded. What we do need is a different take on non-fiction. In many non-fiction tasks, the challenge of meeting the genre requirements is made even more onerous by the need to get your factual information correct. It is far better if we separate the two areas and practise non-fiction skills in a fictional context.

Here's an example from SATs taken by 11 year olds in Britain.

Write a letter to the Council complaining about the swarm of spiders that have invaded your home.

While this task requires a non-fiction format (letter), it is patently fictional work. If we could just spend a short while swapping creepy-crawly anecdotes or doing an 'Invasion of the spiders' drama, then the quality and character of the outcomes would increase greatly.

Of course, we cannot predict test question content and so the chances of having done some relevant drama are very slim. But, imagination is transferable! If pupils are used to making-believe, playing with ideas and empathizing with others, then they will do so easily and instantly, in their own heads, while alone with the paper.

Here's another example.

'Test a rucksack' – Write a report

Less obviously fantasy than the spiders, this still requires real imagination skills to tackle. Children must visualize the rucksack, imagine what it would be like to use it, invent a series of plausible faults or problems. Putting these ideas into a report format is the easy part of the task!

So, why not go the whole way and deliberately teach non-fiction in fantasy settings?

Recount	'What happened while walking through the Dark Woods'
Instructions	How to cover yourself in custard
Report	Life on Planet X
Explanation	How pigs fly
Persuasion	Campaign to ban cheese
Discussion	Should we build our houses out of gingerbread?

Pupils can be engaged and motivated by each and every one of these genres by using the same principles as we have explored in developing literacy through storytelling.

But that's another book entirely...

References

STORYTELLING

Bettelheim, Bruno (1976) *The Uses of Enchantment: the Meaning and Importance of Fairy Tales.* London: Thames and Hudson

Booker, Christopher (2005) *The Seven Basic Plots: Why We Tell Stories.* London: Continuum

Egan, Kieran (1988) *Teaching as Storytelling.* London: Routledge

Estes, Clarissa Pinkola (1992) *Women Who Run with the Wolves: Myths and Stories of the Wild Woman Archetype.* New York: Ballantine

Grainger, Teresa (1997) *Traditional Storytelling in the Primary Classroom.* Leamington Spa: Scholastic

Grugeon, Elizabeth and Gardiner, Paul (2000) *The Art of Storytelling for Teachers and Pupils.* London: David Fulton

Howe, Alan and Johnson, John (1991) *Common Bonds: Storytelling in the Classroom.* London: Hodder and Stoughton

Jennings, Claire (1991) *Children as Storytellers: Developing Language Skills in the Classroom.* Oxford: Oxford University Press

Rosen, Betty (1988) *And None Of It Was Nonsense: the Power of Storytelling in School.* London: Mary Glasgow Publications

Rosen, Betty (1991) *Shapers and Polishers: Teachers as Storytellers.* London: Mary Glasgow Publications

Zipes, Jack (1995) *Fairy Tales and The Art of Subversion.* London: Routledge.

DRAMA

Johnstone, Keith (1999) *Impro for Storytellers.* London: Faber and Faber

Morgan, Norah and Saxton, Juliana (1986) *Teaching Drama.* London: Hutchinson

Wagner, Betty Jane (1979) *Dorothy Heathcote; Drama as a Learning Medium.* London: Hutchinson

Wooland, Brian (1993) *The Teaching of Drama in the Primary School.* London: Longman

VAK, BRAIN-BASED AND ACCELERATED LEARNING

Buzan, Tony (1995) *The Mind Map Book.* London: BBC Books

Edwards, Betty (2001) *The New Drawing on the Right Side of the Brain.* London: Harper Collins

Jensen, Eric (1996) *Brain Based Learning.* Carmarthen: The Accelerated Learning Centre

Hoffman, Eva and Bartkowicz, Zdzistaw *The Learning Adventure.* Learn to Learn

Shaw, Sara and Hawes, Trevor (1998) *Effective Teaching and Learning in the Primary Classroom.* London: DfES

Smith, Alistair *Accelerated Learning in Practice.* Stafford: Network Educational Press

TEACHING LITERACY

Palmer, Sue (2003) *How to teach writing across the curriculum.* London: David Fulton

Corbett, Pie (2002) *How to teach story writing.* London: David Fulton

Index

archetypal plot analysis 115–16

Bettelheim, Bruno, 18–19
blind offers, of imaginary objects 83–4
books, chooser 69
build-up to a story
    headlines/bullet points 109, 111
    storyboards 24, 25, 32–3
    writing frame 127, 129, 130
bullet points 22–3, 37, 42
    and headlines 104–11
    and story transformation 112–14
    and whole-class story-devising 114–15

characters, and storyboarding 37
chooser boards 62–9
    and interactive writing 121–2, 124–5
    preparing for writing 118–20
    retelling stories 62–5
    using in storytelling 65–7
    words on 67–9
chooser books 69
cliff-hanger passing 118
    in collaborative storytelling 86–7
climax to a story
    headlines/bullet points 109, 111
    storyboards 24, 25, 30–2
    writing frame 128, 130
coaching, listening partners 60–2
collaboration
    and writing 102
    whole-class story-devising 114–15
collaborative creativity 80–91
    happy birthday 83–4
    performance skills 84
    show and tell 81–2
    storytelling 85–7
    swaps 80–1
communication
    in the classroom 49–52
    and writing 103
creating storyboards 26–34
creativity 71–96
    imaginary objects 73–7
    imagination versus reality 71–3
    mini dramas 94–6, 133

role play 91–6
    tableaux 87–91, 92
    see also collaborative creativity

direct speech, and storyboards 36
drama, mini dramas 94–6, 133
dynamic nature of storytelling 8

Edwards, Betty, 27
Einstein, Albert 19
EPOGI (educational principle of great
    importance) 78
Estes, Clarissa Pinkola 19
eye contact, and storytelling 8, 10

facial expressions
    storyboards 36
    storytelling 11, 12
fairytales 135
    retelling using chooser boards 62–5
    and story transformation 40
    and storytelling 18–19
    see also Little Red Riding Hood
feedback, and interactive writing 122,
    126
flexibility, and storytelling 8, 9
freeze-framing 90–1, 92, 96
full stops, preparation for writing 118

gestures
    and storyboards 36
    and storytelling 10, 12
gifts, of imaginary objects 82–3
good listeners 46–7, 49, 133
gossiping 18

handwriting 103–4
happy birthday exercise 83–4
headlines 105–11
hearing, and listening 45–6
here it is! exercise 84
hot seating 91–4
    paired 92–4
    teacher in role 91–2, 95, 96
imaginary objects
    blind offers of 83–4

here it is! exercise 84
show and tell exercise 81–2
swapping 80–1
see also magic bags
imagination
and storytelling 8, 9
non-fiction 137
versus reality 71–3
interactive nature of storytelling 9
interactive whiteboards, and
storyboarding 29–30, 33
interactive writing 120–6
chooser boards 121–2, 124–5
and feedback 122
fourth sentence 125–6
mixed-ability groups 120
opening sentences 121
pairings 120, 121–2
second sentences 123–4
third sentences 124
transferring to paper 124, 126
on whiteboards 122–6, 133
interviews, hot seating 91–4
introduction to stories
headlines 111
storyboards 24, 30
writing frame 127, 129

Johnstone, Keith, 72
Jooan Choy storyboard 31

learning, and writing 98–9
listening 45–69
games 46–9
good listeners 46–7, 49, 133
and hearing 45–6
and literacy 14, 15
mantra 48
and speaking 49–52
listening partners 48, 52–8
coaching 60–2
finding a partner 53–4
listening 55
preparation for writing 118
reporting back 57–60
response sandwich 59–60
speaking 55–7
and storyboards 36
literacy, and storytelling 12–16
Little Red Riding Hood

chooser board 65
collaborative retelling 87
DVD 5, 9, 26
headlines/bullet points 107–8, 110, 111
mini drama 94, 95, 96
paired hot seating 92–3
story transformation 78, 112–14
storyboard 30, 32, 36
transformed 116–17
tableau 88–90
writing frame 132
see also Zip Electron

magic bags 73–80
gifts from 82–3
for learning parts of speech 79–80
setting a challenge 77–8
magic microphones 87
marking, and writing frames 131–2
meta coaching, listening partners 61–2
microphones, magic 87
mini dramas 94–6, 133
mixed-ability groups, and interactive
writing 120

National Curriculum 12
National Literacy Strategy 13, 21, 69
non-fiction storytelling 136–7
non-verbal communication, and literacy
15

objects
interviewing inanimate objects 93–4
see also imaginary objects
open questions 63
ownership, and storytelling 8, 9

paired hot seating 92–4
parts of speech, magic bags for learning
79–80
performance skills, and collaborative
creativity 84
pictures, and storyboards 23–4
plot analysis
archetypal 115–16
and storyboards 34–4
punctuation 21, 22
pupils
attitudes to writing 100–1
and teacher attention 50

questions
  open questions 63
  teachers asking 50–1, 64–5

reading, and literacy 14, 15
reality versus imagination 71–3
resolution of a story
  headlines/bullet points 111
  storyboards 24, 25, 30
  writing frame 128, 131
response sandwich 59–60
retelling stories, using chooser boards
  62–5
role play 91–6
  everyone in role drama 95–6
  hot seating 91–4
  teacher in role 91–2, 95, 96

scaffolding 102, 111
self-talk, and literacy 15
SEN pupils 42–4
sentences
  writing 21, 22, 118–20
    interactive 121–6
show and tell exercise 81–2
speaking
  and listening 49–52
  and literacy 14, 15
  see also listening partners
speech bubbles 32, 123
spelling 21, 22, 103–4
  and interactive writing 126
Story Tag 87
story transformation 112–14
  storyboards 37–44
storyboards 12, 21–44, 133
  build-up 24, 25, 32–3
  characters 37
  climax 24, 25, 30–2
  and collaborative storytelling 86
  creating 26–34
    new stories 35
  ending/epilogue 25, 30
  introduction 24, 30
  and pictures 23–4
  plot 37
  preparation and support for telling 35
  resolution 24, 25, 30
  retelling from 36
  Sam's journey 42–4

settings 37
speech bubbles 32
story stages 24–6
success criteria chart 36
transformed 116–17
transforming stories 37–44
  at KS1 39–40
  at KS2 40–1
  uses of 34–5
  visualizing 26–9
  and writing 21–3
  written versions of 33–4
  see also chooser boards
storytelling 7–19
  choosing good words 11
  collaborative 85–7
  dynamic nature of 8
  and eye contact 8, 10
  and facial expressions 11, 12
  fairytales 18–19
  and flexibility 8, 9
  gestures 10, 12
  and gossiping 18
  and imagination 8, 9
  interactive nature of 9
  and listening 49
  and literacy 12–16
  non-fiction 136–7
  and ownership 8, 9
  suspense 11
  teachers as storytellers 11–12
  techniques 9–11
  voices 10
  and writing 16–18
  see also chooser boards
storytelling challenge 120
success criteria charts 133
  good listening 47, 55, 57
  storyboards 36
suspense, and storytelling 11
swapping imaginary objects 80–1
Sweeney, Dai 129

tableaux 87–91
  freeze-framing 82, 90–1, 96
  and interactive writing 123
  and paired hot seating 92
  vivante 90
teachers
  lines of communication in the

classroom 49–52
in role 91–2, 95, 96
as storytellers 11–12
teaching sequence 99, 133
teaching writing 99–101
thinking, and listening 48
Tommy Trevorrow storyboard 31
transformed storyboards 116–17
transforming stories 37–8

visual communication, and listening 47
visualizing, creating storyboards 26–9
voices, and storytelling 10

whiteboards
creating storyboards on 27–9
interactive 29–30, 33
and interactive writing 121–6, 133
whole-class story-devising 114–15
words
on chooser boards 67–9
and storytelling
choosing good words 11
collaborative 85–6
word objectives in writing 118–20
writing 97–132
archetypal plot analysis 115–16
aural preparation for 117–20
word and sentence objectives 118–20

bullet points 22–3, 37, 42, 104–11
creating a positive writing culture
101–4
as difficult 98, 100
frames 126–31, 133
goalposts 103
handwriting 103–4
headlines 105–11
and learning 98–9
less is more in 102, 117–18
and literacy 12–16
principles for an effective writing
culture 97–104
spelling 103–4
story transformation 112–14
and storyboarding 21–3
and storytelling 16–18
support for 102
teaching 99–101
transformed storyboards 116–17
whole-class story-devising 114–15
see also interactive writing

Zip Electron
interactive writing 120–6
story transformation 112–14
transformed storyboard 116–17
whole-class story devising 114–15